OUR PRIDE

OUR PRIDE

Eds. Robinson & Villaseñor

2022

Global Words press

This trade paperback original is published by Global Words Press, Nottingham, England.

This is a work of fiction and non-fiction. For the fiction pieces, names, characters, and incidents are the product of the author's imagination or are used fictitiously. Any resemblance to actual persons, living or dead, business establishments, events, or locales is entirely coincidental. With regards the non-fiction, while all the events in these pieces are true, some names have been changed to protect the privacy of the people involved.

Cataloguing information
ISBN: 978-1-911272-21-2
Credits
Editors: Nicci Robinson & Victoria Villaseñor
Jacket Design: Nicci Robinson
Production Design: Global Wordsmiths
Cover Image: KC Lylark

Foreword

Nottingham and Nottinghamshire enjoy a rich and varied history of providing a safe and supportive environment, indeed a home, for groups traditionally marginalised by society: asylum seekers and refugees, immigrants as well as people of all faiths (and none), of all ethnicities, ages, genders, abilities, sexual orientations, and gender identities. As a city and a county, we are proud to be known as the "Queen of the Midlands," in reference to our role as a champion and advocate for the LGBT+ community–a community which is valued and adds to the rich tapestry of diversity that being part of our city and county offers. However, as you will learn, peoples' experiences of feeling valued, welcomed, and included vary considerably, which you will learn more of as you read.

Our Integrated Care System (ICS) is made up of partner organisations who span health, social care, and beyond, all with the aim of providing joined-up services that meet individual needs. Services that strive to improve the health and well-being outcomes for those from our diverse communities and which actively address health inequalities.

We first came up with the idea of creating an LGBT+ staff anthology in 2020. We know we have hugely creative staff, and we thought it important to capture and showcase their talent. Besides, our shared experience told us that there was a highly receptive audience eager to learn and understand the diverse lived experiences of our LGBT+ staff.

Global Words press took our vision and made it into a reality, the polished, expertly produced book that you hold in your hands. Professional yet authentic, Nicci and Victoria carefully ensured that they retained the true voice of our staff. The Arts Council also graciously supported the project, and for that, we are truly thankful.

This anthology is made up of stories from LGBT+ staff who work in the Nottingham and Nottinghamshire ICS in roles such as doctors, nurses, midwives, researchers, administrators, psychologists, well-being practitioners, social workers, and more.

We are so proud of them all, and we hope you enjoy reading this anthology as much as we did. Although this is only a small sample of the many stories out there, we believe you will be captivated by the talent, creativity, and passion demonstrated by those who so generously shared their time and talents, who bravely came forward to say, "We're Proud."

Catherine Conchar and Giles Matsell
Joint Equality, Diversity, and Inclusion Leads for the Nottingham and Nottinghamshire ICS

Dedication

This book is dedicated to all the people in the world who are unable to express their pride, and for those in our community who have paid the ultimate price for their difference.

Stories

Stories by Benji Rose Ingall page 1

Dreaming Was My Prerequisite by James Brown page 3

Free Love by Sam Stormborn page 11

My Gender by Rebecca Summerscales page 13

Hidden in Plain Sight by Jamie Taylor page 15

A Moment of Hope by Fern Wood page 21

Gender Pronouns by Andrea (Annie) Alleyne page 27

She by AP Bramley page 29

Dates and Dragons by Elouise Abby page 31

Collecting the A's by Renee Fischer page 37

Declaration of Love by Vanessa Ball page 43

Humpback Whales by Saffron Sage page 45

Lost and Found by Hazel Clark page 47

Hindsight Is a Wonderful Thing by Jamie Mann page 59

To Eat a Starving Dog by Rebecca Summerscales page 79

The Dinner Party by Laura Martin page 81

Hostile by Saffron Sage page 95

People Tell You by Fern Wood page 97

As Far as I've Come by Vanessa Ball page 99

The Journey by Saffron Sage page 109

Finite Forgiveness by AP Bramley page 113

Out and Proud by Andrea (Annie) Alleyne page 115

Tits by Sara Gray page 117

You're Such a Good Pup by Pup Teddy page 131

Jen by Tray Morgan page 137

Soulmate by Saffron Sage page 139

The Conversation by Tray Morgan page 143

A Life in the Wrong Body by Sam Stormborn page 153

Your Truest Nature by Vanessa Ball page 155

My Father's Son by AP Bramley page 157

My Progress by P-Shell page 169

Stories

Benji Rose Ingall

As surely as my body consists of stardust, my soul consists of stories. I am an amalgamation of everyone I have ever loved.

I have stories of cave rescues. The adrenaline, the structured calm, the harmony of a group working in unity.

I have stories of strong handshakes and of isolated adventures, deep in the bowels of the earth. The impenetrable darkness, the unforgiving cold which seeps bone deep. The ways the strange sounds of the stone labyrinths echo and distort. The indescribable, exquisite structures which appear to have been carved by the hand of a master, the feeling of laying your eyes upon massive scenes of extreme natural beauty, and knowing you are the first to see this offering of mother nature.

I have stories of pirate radio and of gem shops.

I have stories of attic railways, the sharp pain of the cold metal ladder on my chubby young hands, the smell of cold, and dust, and brick. The way the lights flicker before committing to illumination, revealing the beautiful mountainside town, trains weaving in and out of caves on their tiny tracks. Miniature cows grazing by a river, miniature people waving from a Ferris wheel.

I have stories of the love of an actress and a stagehand.

I have stories of Christmases given over to saving lives, celebrating on the eve or Boxing Day so we could be together.

I have stories which hide in gruff voices, in the smell of whisky and pipe tobacco, in the gritty feeling of beach sand in the bottom of the bathtub.

I have stories of casseroles, a deep and powerful flavour, bowls and bowls consumed as we squatted on the cardboard flooring between piles of belongings, the warmth penetrating my heart, the recipe now lost to the universe.

I have stories of the colour green, of molecules connecting, of rainbows trapped in lakes. Of laughing together in lightning storms, running through the rain, of hearts connected and filled with joy.

I have stories of sugar cane, the feeling of ripping the bark with my back teeth, the sweetness of the juices, the brown stains running down my arms.

I have stories of a desperate love for life, dance, and song resonating with the acceptance of inevitable and premature death.

I have stories of fire, of disease, of heartbreak.

I have so many stories, and yet none of them are mine to tell. They are the stories of the people I love, the people who have made me. I cannot tell them to you, but I don't need to. They are your stories. They are everyone's stories, in every place, in every time. They are the stories told around the campfire, and they are the stories told on the biggest of screens. They are the stories of love and of loss, and they are the only stories which have ever been told.

Dreaming Was My Prerequisite

James Brown

PICTURE THIS: THE OVEN you now call home continuously blasts hot rays that enrich your ebony skin, and you love it; sweat seeping from the top of your head is unrestricted in its descent, because your eyebrows are shaved monthly; clothing is restricted to deep-ochre, rectangular cloth that enshrines your baking body, and the rhythmic cadence of the Northeast Thai dialect is something you're still trying to perfect.

My one-way ticket to Thailand originated from my mighty desire for enlightenment, spiritual ascension, transcendence, or however else you would like to describe not wanting to follow the typical milestones societies exalt. Not because I wanted to be edgy or was non-conformist, per se, but when I had just finished university, the painful chasm between my holding the posh-looking certificate and the mental anguish I had endured wasn't something I could ignore. If *that* level of stress made me feel *that* frazzled, something not even a certificate with my name could ameliorate, then I had to redress my priorities.

This led me on a search to meditate far, far away from my hometown of Nottingham. It's funny, because this determination to prioritise my own well-being gave me unparalleled levels of strength and courage, plain and simple gutsy, grittiness that I would, in years to come, hanker after. This courage, for example, allowed me to face my fear of flying. Binge-watching years of air crash investigation documentaries with my mum hadn't left me feeling confident about being in a tin can in the sky. And yet, I did four silent meditation retreats across Thailand. It was during my second retreat in 2014 that I had my first sneak peek into the nourishing depths meditation affords. It made my resolve resolute. Focusing on plunging further into the abyss of meditation and therefore my own spiritual and mental well-being became my bullseye.

In February 2016, I was ordained as a Buddhist monk. The Thai Forest tradition, with its emphasis on the ascetic way of living in forests, like the times of the Buddha, was optimal for ensuring mindfulness was maintained continuously. The array of venomous snakes, giant centipedes, huntsman spiders (whose characteristics are perfectly described by their name), and deceptively innocent scorpions meant that losing focus could have adverse consequences. To constantly be aware of my outside environment spilt into constantly being aware of my inside environment.

Though being surrounded by these wild creatures wasn't my favourite aspect of living in the forest, I wore the privilege and gratitude everywhere I went. I mean, how often do you get an opportunity like that? Not being employed, my sole job was to work on and develop my mind. Not having a sexual relationship, my sole relationship was with myself so I could purify my mind. Not enjoying what materialism and consumerism had to offer, I bathed in the serene sounds of quietude and wildlife. I relished my new home so much and felt a constant connection to a lineage established millennia ago. I was living a life that was compatible with my core value of self-development and, consequently, the unpleasant animals I was living amongst were a blot on the skyscraper of my meditative living. It was a drastic change from holding my bachelor's degree certificate back in the UK, where my purpose hadn't yet been activated.

I had been ordained for a little over a year, and my routine was generally solid. I would tend to be the first monk to wake up at 4:30 a.m., don my formal attire with my right shoulder exposed, and make my way out of my wooden hut through the winding paths of the forest to the meeting hall. My vision extended only to the perimeter of the torch light. Raucous cicadas, communicating in harmony, made it difficult to listen for animals on the forest floor. Having now been accustomed to seeing mile-long snakes thud to the ground from trees, my wish routinely revolved around wanting night vision. Once I arrived at the meeting hall, I slammed the mallet into the mammoth gong four times. I can still feel those reverberations in my body today. Slowly but surely, the community of monks and nuns would gather for chanting, meditation, and the hallmark of Buddhist monastic communities, alms round.

We would all walk barefoot around the nearby villages, monks in one direction and nuns in another, collecting food freely given by Buddhist followers. Sticky rice and meat dishes were guaranteed, and sickly-sweet treats were a regular occurrence. This day started off as a regular one. The constant battle between me and my sweet tooth was hard-won by the latter. In contrast to a mindfully meditative monk, with discipline upholding good all-around conduct, I heaped my bowl with sugary delights.

At this stage, having spent over a year eating one main meal a day around eight a.m., my stomach had shrunk in capacity, and I could only eat so much in one sitting. Ringing between my ears was what my mum would always say if we took too much food, and it was true. My eyes *were* bigger than my belly. I was *stuffed*!

What followed was a peculiar day that I would seldom tell people about for years to come. I encountered an adverse consequence of an unusual kind. No, another snake didn't drop from a tree, nor did mosquitoes retire from their ferocious feeding frenzy; it was something downright strange. You see, a few basic behaviours assist "bhāvanā" or the development of meditation. Overeating is a fast way of entering into what the Thai locals jokingly rephrased as "bhāva norn" or the development of sleeping meditation. It was the combination of stifling heat and a stomach practically on the verge of exploding which resulted in an express ticket to unbridled sleep. I returned to my hut to get full use out of my ticket.

The rusty-brown sleeping tent acted as refuge from the mosquitoes, though their irritatingly high-pitched noise abounded in my hut. Like a patient listening to a surgeon count down from ten, I drifted into my private affair with my dream-world within seconds of laying on the stiff wooden slats.

I was beamed into a fast-food restaurant and was a silent witness to a worker handling some French fries. It was as though I was hovering directly over his shoulder, but he didn't detect my presence. The scrumptiously sizzling oil and bright marigold-coloured French fries were immediately captivating. Perhaps it was the incandescent hues that effortlessly pushed away the drabness of the stainless steel fryer. The fragrance added a halo to the scene that made me wonder whether I had died and gone to heaven. Something for certain, however, was that the sunshine radiance of this pleasing view automatically filled my *entire* being with joy.

During my surge of dreamy well-being, the heat flirted with my taste buds. Please bear in mind that my one meal a day consisted of food that was no warmer than room temperature. The worker continued with what I can only describe as alchemy and lovingly lavished crystals of tiny white gems over the golden strands of tastiness. Again, the last time a French fry hit my tongue was back in England over a year ago. My gaze zoomed in on the unfolding scene before me. Molecular details limited my entire vista to the perfect pairing: a tantalisingly hot French fry laced with pristine, white salt. Bearing witness to the perfect couple was torturous; I just *had* to interrupt the ceremony.

I have no recollection of how it happened, but a few salty French fries ended up in my mouth. Doing so was instinctive. Feeling hot food on my tongue transformed my frazzled inner landscape into an oasis. My soul burst into full bloom as the French fries quenched my thirst for a much-missed snack. The excitement, however, was too much...

An unusual substance–an old acquaintance–wrenched me from my dreamy sphere back into my kiln-heated reality. Suddenly, my headiness tumbled into stifling shame. My thighs were signed by a sticky and hot outpouring brought about by the dream. I rose in bewilderment. Putting two and two together led to a multitude of questions. Am I weird? Do I really love fries that much? Will this happen again? This hasn't happened since puberty. Am I normal? You name it, I thought it!

With waning drowsiness, I unzipped my tent and reached for something to wipe off the embarrassing explosion. Soon after, I squatted next to my toilet to hand-wash my robe whilst toying with telling my teacher what had happened. After all, he was there to give me guidance on anything and everything, though he would typically give pithy statements that allowed me to chew the cud in my own time.

And that's exactly what happened. After winding my way down to his hut, I conformed to not only monastic rules but also to Thai social rules of paying respect to elders. Kneeling before him with my hands palm-to-palm in front of my chest, I raised them to my forehead then bowed my forehead to the ground three times. His gracefully gentle grin greeted me when I'd finished paying respects, and then I sat with my feet tucked to one side (in Thailand, pointing your feet at somebody is disrespectful). As I held my hands in front of my chest, I delivered my experience peppered with embarrassing frankness. He offered comfort, and reassurance, and dissolved my fears that I had done something awful. His advice was simple: to moderate the amount I eat and, when I felt tired after a meal, do walking meditation. With a light body and mind, I paid my respects once again and left my teacher's hut.

However healing his words of advice were for my situation, and indeed they were comforting and helpful, flickers of intrigue slowly ignited into a hunt for knowledge about what I could unpack from this dream. It was so odd, so spectacular, and so abnormal that I couldn't let it go. I felt like it meant something more, something I wasn't seeing.

Flashbacks of the dream jolted me over the following days. It was clear that I had to focus on why it had such an impact on me. So instead of using my breathing as my anchor for meditation, I suspended it in place of contemplating and examining the minute chronology of the dream, much like a coroner would do.

Being a monk, you renounce, to a large extent, the freedom to choose what you eat and when you eat. Whilst in Thailand, there wasn't a single soul that I missed, not a friend, family member, or ex-colleague whose company I craved. That's not to say that I didn't love my friends and family; I did and still do. However, what was both surprising and stark for me was how much I missed food. Whether it was a greasily juicy kebab hugged by garlic mayo or a simple but underrated cheese and onion pasty, food was my Achilles heel. I would often think about it, and the fact I couldn't cook (as monk rules preclude this) meant that sometimes my imagination ran wild when I saw laypeople cooking with utensils and ingredients I never knew existed. Dreaming about fast food had reminded me of something I had long missed, and my burning desire to smack it in my mouth was the bare bones of the dream. But there was more to it. Dreaming about food isn't strange. Getting excited about food isn't strange. Getting *that* excited about food, to me, is strange. Balancing on the boundaries of not strange and strange was the next step of my inquiry.

Of note, over many months I had practiced a meditation technique that focused on the four elements of earth, wind, fire, and water. Earth represents hardness/softness, wind represents movement, fire represents hot and cold temperatures, and water represents fluidity. This technique looks at every single material object in the entire universe, French fries included, through the exact same lens of how they express each element. This technique came in handy for my examination of the dream, because it allowed me to get over the embarrassing aspect of that particular food having such an effect on me. No longer was I regurgitating the dream with embarrassment, because the four elements technique extinguished the labels humans give to objects and put them all on a level playing field.

Rewinding the dream from start to finish illuminated a couple of oversights. If I had been dreaming about a person, then my original embarrassment would likely have been less severe. Dreaming about a person I desired/missed would also make more sense, because I've never had a food fetish. To make this dream make sense, I experimented with replacing the food with a human being. Remember, they are both nameless objects that *only* differ on their expression of their four characteristics when using those elements to view reality. My inquiry started an internal shift.

I then picked up on another oversight. My way of thinking or way of describing what I was seeing in the dream led me to appreciate that this specific process added fuel to my fire. No wonder there was an explosion! It's not the case that I was passively seeing the French fries being doused with salt; my mind was an active participant in thinking about what I was seeing. I thought the fries looked divine, the sight of them caused me to think about how much I'd missed eating them, and I was super eager to guzzle them and see how they tasted. They were all thoughts along very similar streams of thinking in my dream. Breaking it down like that was revolutionary to me because, come on, I didn't have much practice holding a mirror up to such a constant and taken for granted process. How often did I examine the nature of my thoughts up until then? Not very often. Because of this, acknowledging this layer was a stepping stone in my inquiry.

Coming up to my mid-twenties, and secluded in a rural Thai forest, I was still in the closet, though I knew I was attracted to my gender from approximately seven. What made me so acutely sensitive to hiding this reality and pretending the opposite was true from that young age? Why did this secrecy persist up to this point in my life? Why did my urges and longings, superficially met via gay porn, keep me from exploring a living, breathing intimacy with a real man? Why was I so afraid? Quietly, dangerously sharp shards of denial and shame slowly but surely crumbled from my core.

And then, it hit me. Going over these stages made the formula so easy. You see an object, you have thoughts about liking it, you crave it, you get it, and there is a physical response because you like it so much. The end. Like the sun banishing away darkness, a glaringly obvious fact had escaped me up until then. This is the exact same process that happens for heterosexual as well as homosexual people. That formula is the way our mind works when interacting with its environment. It was an additional equaliser that made it impossible for me to maintain a sense of shame, denial, and embarrassment about my sexuality. How could it be otherwise when the formula for heterosexuals is the same for me, bar a different object?

This enquiry revolutionised my relationship with myself. Though I was compassionate to others, irrespective of difference—sexuality or otherwise—I'd never given the same level of compassion to myself. Though I was there to support others, I had pushed away and rejected that important part of me. It was an important realisation I would carry with me into the future.

Days crawled into weeks. Weeks strolled into months. Months blossomed into years. No longer was I a monk living in Thailand. Time passed, but the lesson from the dream mulled and matured in my abyss. Lush forest landscapes morphed into concrete buildings.

The enquiry concluded by first changing how I would speak to myself. Rather than force my urges, tinged with shame, to the back of my mind, I quickly learned that I could get comfortable with recognising that desires are normal and human, including homosexual ones. They floated in my conscience and drifted away, eventually to come back again. Perhaps it was an attractive guy on the street that I walked by, or maybe it was a gay porn star I had an imaginary connection with. Whether there was an obvious reason or not, the shame I'd had was well and truly gone. Being rid of this insidious emotion was freeing, to say the least.

One day, whilst in a retail job, a colleague came out to me as bisexual. It was the catalyst for me to confess to him that I was gay, then I came out to friends and eventually, my family. The feeling of freedom and being comfortable with who I am intensified. The iron-clad denial and shame I'd had about my sexuality had long ago crumbled away, and I put it down to the two equalisers of the four elements meditation and the formula. My prerequisite dream allowed me to bathe in the man I am today, proudly loving *and* being loved by a man who is showing me transcendence of another kind.

Free Love

Sam Stormborn

Liberty is a right we should all enjoy,
Guided by our personal choices,
Befriending people from all walks of life,
Taking time to hear everyone's voices.
Questioning the narrow beliefs of some,
Imagining a world that is healing,
Aligning a culture of peace and love,
Plus being open about our feelings.

Fear not the beliefs of others,
Rise above the fear and hate,
Embrace your own identity,
Endeavour to challenge the state.

Live a life that is full and free,
Overcome the fears from within,
Value everyone for who they are,
Enjoying love isn't a sin.

My Gender

Rebecca Summerscales

My gender is dried up tubes of mascara,
3 a.m. YouTube clips of Impractical Jokers.

My gender is street-cleaning machines gurning,
cigarette ends, and dead leaves, pedals on a still bike.

My gender is curtains, not blinds.
It is a running bath with the plug taken out.

My gender is salty fingers from sweat, or snacks.
It is a gentle touch, a foam ball dragged by the wind.

My gender is a white Land Rover, a ticking engine, a sighing tyre.
It is wearing exclusively black nails and ordering binders on Amazon.

My gender is bringing a pen to a sword fight.
My gender is believing a blunt knife is safer than a sharp one.

My gender is emptied jewel casings on cheap shoes—
metal prongs prised open, a hanging jaw, gouged-at eyes.

Hidden in Plain Sight

Jamie Taylor

I SHOULD START THIS narrative by saying I'm now an out and proud part of the LGBTQ+ community, and I'm comfortable being me. I embrace my difference, accept who I am, and look forward to discovering who I'm yet to become. However, that's not always been the case.

Coming out is one of those phrases that as a queer person, I find immensely annoying. To come out suggests an LGBTQ+ person having to hope for acceptance in a cisgendered, hetero-normative world. In the early days of discovering my sexuality, that was my view too; however, as I've grown older and wiser, I see my coming out as giving others the opportunity to come into my life. Less me coming out of the metaphorical closet and more about someone being brought into *my* closet. My closet is like that famous wardrobe that takes you to another land filled with mystical animals, witches, and Turkish delight, except my other land is one filled with rainbow flags, unicorns, way too much glitter, and most importantly, acceptance and tolerance. When I choose to be open with you about my sexuality or gender identity, it signifies I trust you, and I want you to understand that part of me. I've never expected my cis, straight friends and family to tell me they're straight and/or cis. So why is someone who's queer always expected to come out and label themselves to achieve someone else's narrative of happiness and fulfilment? Rant over.

There are three main parts to my coming out story. One: how I came out to my friends; two: how I came out to my peers at college; and three, how I came out to my family. Each one had a different reaction, but I won't put any spoilers here.

Growing up in the northeast of England, I was often surrounded by communities who saw difference as a bad thing. I had no LGBTQ+ role models to look to for inspiration or comfort, leaving me to flounder in my disparate and unregulated thoughts around what normal—and therefore believing I was abnormal—actually looked like.

I'd say I was the stereotypical confused child, going shopping with my parents, not looking twice at the lingerie section but not being able to get enough of the packets and boxes with images of toned, sculptured men in tight Y-fronts. It was safe to say I knew I was different. The further through my childhood I went, the more the feelings of difference echoed in my mind like a rolling voice in an empty cave.

Throughout secondary school, I tried to hide my sexuality. Other pupils asked, as teenagers always do, and often mocked me, but I think I survived with no more of a rough ride than most other kids. I had a great group of friends. We were inseparable and hung out most evenings, either skateboarding or BMXing, going for a walk in the woods near our homes, or just chilling in the local park. By the age of sixteen, I'd had a few girlfriends but nothing particularly serious or meaningful, and nothing ever got sexual. It was my attempt at trying to disown my difference and fit into my heteronormative surroundings.

One evening, when my friends and I were all together in the local park, I decided to come out. This was it–the first time I'd ever voiced to someone else that I was gay. My heart pounding, I said, "Hey, I've got something to tell you all." An eerie silence fell over the starlit park. I told myself, it was now or never. Speaking at a pace I didn't know I could, I blurted out, "I'm sorry, I think I'm gay," and then burst into tears.

Why I felt the need to apologise, I'll never really understand, but I did. I'd built this moment up in my mind, fully expecting that I was probably going to lose my friendship group, and no one would ever want to talk to me again. Sobbing into my hands, seconds felt like hours. I couldn't see anyone but suddenly, I felt arms around me, hugging me, and others cheered and whooped. One of my best friends said, "Finally. We've known for ages." He had a huge grin on his face. They didn't care. They were true friends who accepted me for who I was without even a second thought. It felt amazing. I felt lighter, happier, confident. I kept crying, but the feeling behind the tears was one of relief and happiness, rather than anguish and fear.

***

Starting college in a different town was a big eye-opener. The campus I studied at also ran the hair and beauty courses. All the guys on those courses were stereotypically gay. Flamboyance seemed to be a prerequisite although secretly, I wasn't complaining. I hadn't come out to my college friends yet. My friends at home were amazing, loyal, and inclusive, but this was a new group of people. Some of the lads on my course made comments about the guys on the hair and beauty courses, which gave me even less reason to come out. I'd gone from feeling confident, understood, and accepted to living a parallel life once again, trying to pass as straight. Internally, it was torturous not knowing if I was going to be outed.

However, I plucked up the courage to come out about halfway through my first year. Huddled under the smoking shelter one lunchtime, and with no one else around except my best friend, I thought it was a perfect time to say something. With a deep breath and a slightly sick feeling in my stomach, I told her. She made a squeaking noise akin to a small mouse, hugged me and then, like my friends at home, said, "I've known for ages but didn't want to ask. I've seen how you look at those beauty course boys." She gave me a look that said, "Go get them, tiger."

At this point, I realised that I was clearly useless at hiding my sexuality. Everyone else seemed to know, despite my best efforts. Did I have a big, fluorescent sign that said, "This person is gay" floating above my head? Another couple of students from our course came outside and with far too much excitement, my friend told them. They were also fine about it. We went to the corner shop to buy more cigarettes and unbeknownst to me, my friends bought balloons. On the walk back to college, they blew them up, wrote, "Congrats, you're gay" on them, and tied them to my bag. It was both hugely embarrassing and an easy way to gain the attention of the boys in hair and beauty. As the saying goes, there's no such thing as bad publicity, right?

Turns out, there is. Standing tall, chest out, and my best queer foot forward, I walked happily through the college canteen and onwards to afternoon lectures. However, the bountiful joy wasn't to last. That afternoon we had advanced physiology and our lecturer, although generally lovely, was old-school. He asked what the balloons were for and before my brain could conjure up a believable, rational reason for them, my friend impulsively blurted out, "He's come out to us today."

Her smile faded slowly as a deafening silence engulfed the room. All eyes flitted between me and the lecturer as if we were playing a game of invisible tennis. My lecturer finally said, "It's just a phase. No one can really be like that." And with that, on we went with the afternoon's lecture. My heart sank. Feeling deflated and like an oddity at a circus show with everyone staring at me, I shoved my bag under the desk and said nothing. It was my first experience of overt homophobia. I wanted the floor to swallow me up. No amount of hand-holding or supportive looks from friends around the room could make it any better.

I used to share a lift with one of the guys on my course. He'd pick me up and drop me off a couple of days a week. At the end of the day, I said that I'd see him in the usual place the following morning. He told me he didn't know I was gay, and he now felt uncomfortable being in the car alone with me. My initial thought was that he'd be lucky to have me make a move on him, but my passive-aggressive inner voice soon turned to anger, confusion, sadness, and betrayal. And that was that. After six months of college, he hardly spoke to me again, and when he did, I was never on my own. Having never experienced any anti-gay comments before, I'd now endured two in the space of a few hours.

So, off I walked to the bus, feeling empty and alone. Why had I said anything? While my metaphorical closet was a lonely place, it was a safe space. After that day, it felt more like a rickety old barn door covered in cracks, and it no longer felt quite as safe as it had. And yet, being out didn't feel safe either.

***

After finishing college in August 2006, I wasn't starting university until the May of the following year, giving me a ten-month break. Along with two friends, we decided to go to Australia for three weeks. I hadn't told my parents that I was gay. I loved them, and they loved me, but I was more than a little anxious that they wouldn't accept me, and it would be one of those things that was never spoken about again. Do I tell them before I go to Australia? But if they're upset with me, that would ruin my holiday. Do I tell them when I get back? I'll worry the whole holiday then, because I know the time has come.

On the plane to Australia, we had plenty of time to talk about it–thirty-four hours, to be precise! That's it, I decided; I was going to tell them. Getting off the plane, I texted them to say I was safe in Australia, I was gay, and that I smoked. My theory being, tell them everything and then deal with one massive implosion of anger, disappointment, or abandonment all at once. I made sure I finished the message with two x's... I don't know why. Perhaps the idealist in me thought this would soften the blow. And with that, I turned my phone off for three weeks. I'd told them, but I couldn't face the response.

Just before leaving Australia on the homeward flight, I knew I needed to text my mum to say we were on time on the plane. Tentatively, I turned my phone back on to find a text from my mum. Shit! I'd blanked it out over the last few weeks, and the reality that I had to deal with this was like a right hook from a heavyweight boxer. I opened the message.

Thanks for telling us. We love you no matter what. Just stop smoking.

The relief that they didn't hate me and I still had a place to go home to was amazing. My parents collected the three of us from the airport. My mum gave me a huge hug, a kiss, and simply said, "I love you." Everything was fine.

My coming out journey continues, as it's not a static point in time. Every time I talk about my partner, people make assumptions about my sexuality. Every time I talk about gender identity and my pronouns, people ask me why. Being completely honest with myself, I think I quite enjoy being ambiguous, disowning labels, and keeping people guessing, but that's just my wily and mischievous personality coming to the surface. Coming out is a lifelong process, but I'm in a place where I'm content with being me and being a proud non-conformist part of the queer community. And I love it. For anyone out there worried about the reaction of those around them, just remember, it's often not as bad as you think. And for those times when people can't or won't accept you for being you, be proud and own your identity. You deserve better, and there will always be a space for you in the LGBTQ+ community.

A Moment of Hope

Fern Wood

I'M GOING TO MY mother's for dinner. I don't exactly dislike my mum, but there's always a change that I need to make to be around her. Changing yourself for an environment comes at a price. Some wordless, indescribable price. It could be a nice stomach ulcer brewing in the years to come. It could be buying ten cats and only leaving the house for cat food (which did slightly appeal to me).

"Hi, Mum," I said, walking into the house and kissing her on the cheek.

"Emma, there you are! I have loads of stories to tell you," she said, smiling broadly and not quite taking her eyes off the cooker in front of her.

I looked out the window at the world around me. There was a red river with an oily sheen going past the house. The wind that blows for three hours per day, every day, was just finishing its shift, and the dusty purple soil that covered the world was getting ready to settle for the evening. I could just make out my reflection in the window with my blue eyes, long lashes, and squat neck. It reminded me of my pledge last week to really get stuck into my diet, before I swiftly forgot and ordered a pizza when I couldn't be bothered with dinner.

I tuned back in to my mum just as she finished a story about the people that had been in the library that week, and I felt a swirl of guilt that I'd missed basically everything she'd said. She looked happy though, and I was pleased to see that she had found some peace in her new job.

"How are things with you? Any updates on your job?" she asked.

"It's all right, thanks. The children can't wait for half-term to start, so they haven't done much work this week," I said. I work in a local school, a five-minute walk from my house, a five-minute walk from my childhood home. I like children but would also just about manage if I never saw another child again.

"And what about that man you talked about? Have you seen each other again?" she asked.

"No. I felt a little uncomfortable, so we haven't been out again," I said.

There was a long, pregnant pause, one that spoke loudly but was never verbalised.

Those pauses had started when I was in primary school. I'd been around ten years old, and our friend group was just getting to the age of giggling about our crushes. A new girl had started at school and for the first time in my life, I felt that I might be able to contribute to the conversation. However, I didn't get the response I'd hoped for, and after the silence, came the report to the teacher, and then the phone calls to my parents, resulting in silence wherever I went.

I quickly understood that being gay wasn't tolerated in my town, and I felt very alone for a long time.

Throughout this time, I had listened to the boys call me a lesbian over and over, as if it was the world's worst insult.

I heard the stories about that one person in school who was open about their sexuality trying to hang himself, because he couldn't be open *and* accepted. I watched him walk around the school, always alone. I wanted to speak to him, but I was scared he wouldn't respond well. And it was easy to tell myself that we weren't both stuck in our own loneliness, to allow myself to just not get involved.

I bit my tongue when the beautiful and only transgender woman in town was chased out of bars, too extreme to exist where other people could see her.

I turned off the TV whenever the stories included gay men and women, just as my mum had taught me.

How disgusting it was to be different, I was told. And although that opened a chasm of sadness in my soul, and no matter how much it felt like a betrayal, I learned to accept what I was told.

And that's how things stayed for too long. I hid who I was from the world and from myself. I kept my head down and didn't look people in the eye, afraid they'd see past the flimsy wall I'd built to hide how different I was. But then, my life began to change.

I'd walked into the lunch hall and looked around, whilst also not wanting to draw attention to myself. I'd just started teaching school and had moved out of my parents' house. I smiled at the thought of what had already changed since I'd moved. I could live at my own speed and had spent two days painting my walls with whatever colours I wanted. My life was my own, and my time was mine to spend, and it gave me a new layer of confidence that I was in control.

However, some things hadn't changed. I sat down at a table and prepared to eat alone, just as I had throughout my school days. I saw people around me I might be able to develop friendships with, but I still felt just on the periphery. With the increased freedom, I started to want things for myself that I hadn't for a long time, like being able to be my absolute true self. I just wasn't sure how to begin.

"Can I sit here?" someone asked.

I looked up, startled. I saw a beautiful person looking back at me. She had long braids, which seemed to sparkle in the sunlight. She had a relaxed gait and an easy smile that spread to her eyes, bright green and framed by a fan of lashes.

"Of...of course," I said, my voice an octave higher than normal, and I congratulated myself on acting like a pre-pubescent child. She settled down in the chair next to me with no awkwardness in sitting so close or in meeting my gaze.

I had never seen anyone who looked like her. Her outfit, bright blue and pink, stood out like a flower in the lunch hall of black clothes, an unwritten regulation. People around her were muttering and back at home, she would have been talked about, intimidated, and mocked into either conforming or being outcast into obscurity.

She wasn't the most conventionally beautiful, symmetrical, or thin person. But I thought she was spectacular.

"I noticed you in orientation earlier," she said, "and I wanted to come and introduce myself. I'm Ric, short for Veronica."

"Oh..." I said, a little shocked that I hadn't seen her, but she'd seen me. "I'm Emma."

"Emma. Are you going to the beginning of the course party tonight?"

"I'm not sure. I think so," I said.

"I'll look out for you," she said. She stood up and walked away, giving me a wave.

I spent the rest of the day thinking about her. About her smile, her laugh, the way she really looked at me when we were talking. My stomach was a whirlwind of butterflies. By the time my three house-mates and I left the house, I was a mess of nerves.

I walked into the club, last in line, attempting not to catch anyone's eyes and trying to get used to the loud music.

They danced, flirted, and drank, and I stayed with them until I had to take a break, and when I returned, they'd gone. I tried to blink down tears and walked around, wanting to leave but not wanting to leave without seeing Ric.

And there she was. She made her own path through the dancing bodies, with people instinctively moving out of the way of her commanding presence.

She wore a white outfit that stood out against her skin and seemed to float around her curves. She was tall already but with heels, she reached six feet and showed not one hint of being self-conscious about being the tallest person in the room. Weren't women supposed to be delicate? A voice that sounded like my mother, my teacher, and everyone from my past whispered in my ear. I felt torn between my own thoughts of admiration and the poisonous mutterings. Surely someone like her couldn't be *wrong*.

"Hi, Emma," she said, and somehow, I heard her over the music.

She carried two drinks and offered one to me. I took it without caring what it was.

We stood looking at each other for a beat before she gestured to the outside bar where it was quieter, and we took a seat opposite each other.

"Where are you from?" I asked, eager to offer something more to the interaction than just staring at her.

"East Handover, but I've moved around most of my life."

She talked about her family, living with her sisters and her dad, and she seemed sad. I wanted to ask her more, but she leaned over and tucked a stray piece of hair behind my ear. I was a little shocked about the casual touch, when touch had so rarely been part of my life. I raised my hand to the spot her fingers had just left.

She leaned towards me. "So what about you?" she asked.

"I'm extremely boring," I said, without thinking. "I mean, I've just moved here from Nughet for teacher training. I've never lived anywhere else."

"I'm sure you're not boring," she said, and a slow smile spread across her face. "Favourite TV series?"

"Spacemaster," I said, slightly too tipsy to think of a better response than the truth.

"Same here," she said, her eyes glittering with approval. "But I didn't like the latest season."

We relaxed into an argument about which actor was best, which made me laugh, and my heart beat faster as I watched her expressions change when she was passionate about something.

"And what about your sexuality?" she asked.

I paused, thrown off by the question and my lack of a prepared response to it. I looked around to check no one was listening. No one had ever asked about what I thought about my own sexuality. No one had ever given me a choice. "I...I don't know," I said slowly, looking at the table. "You?"

"Well, I'm pansexual, but I first thought I was bisexual. I came out when I was fifteen, and it's felt right ever since then."

She spoke so confidently, like it was something that was part of her and that she liked it even. How did that feel? I couldn't imagine.

"Come with me," she said, suddenly standing up and offering her hand.

I took it. Her hand was smooth, and she laced her fingers through mine. My stomach tumbled and lurched with nerves and hopefulness. I didn't care where we were going as long as I was going with her.

We walked out of the club and down an alleyway. I started to become uneasy as we walked, and I realised that no one actually knew where I was, and I didn't know my way around well enough to reliably find my way back.

However, just as I was about to release her hand from mine and turn around, we stopped in front of a black door. She opened it confidently and behind it stood a man wearing eyeliner and blusher, expertly applied.

"Hi, Ric," he said. "Six pounds, as always, and the new one can come in for free." He winked at me.

We walked through the doors. I had never seen anywhere that looked so magical; the walls shimmered and glowed, and I knew this was something special.

Two drag performers stood on stage, beautifully made up and moving together through their routine. I saw men holding hands and staring into each other's eyes, women dancing together, and other people who wanted to be here, claiming their space in the world.

My eyes filled with tears as I looked around at the colours and glitter and people existing together in the form that they felt comfortable in. And as my heart filled with hope, I thought that maybe I could find myself here as well. I let Ric lead me to the dance floor, knowing my life would never be the same.

Gender Pronouns

Andrea (Annie) Alleyne

Gender pronouns ... gender pronouns ... such subjective words.
Gender pronouns ... gender pronouns ... loaded nouns, not verbs.
Words can hurt and words can heal,
Words have the power to affect how you feel.

Don't assume you know someone or can tell their gender just by looking at them.
Don't assume a person wants to go by the most common pronouns she/her, he/him.
People are individuals, beings like no one else, and
People shouldn't be defined by what they want to call themselves.
Instead, judge a person by their character and good deeds,
Not by their gender pronouns, their sexuality, faith, or creed.

Gender pronouns... gender pronouns ... something that should never be assumed.
Gender pronouns...gender pronouns ... something to be respected, not abused.
Better to check the pronouns that each and every person prefers.
Better to enquire with sincerity, to avoid any unintended slurs.

He/him/his, she/her/hers, they/them/theirs, so much more than merely words.
Respect, validation, and inclusion; not stereotypes and alienation.
Identity, choice, and freedom are rights that should be afforded to everyone!

She

AP Bramley

She is a collection of memories
Of connections and titles
Of achievements and tests
Etched into bones that creak
Under the weight of her legacy

She is an ill-fitting dress
That looks perfectly tailored
They don't see the sandpaper stitches
Or the pins in the skin
Holding the fabric in place

She is a stormy cloud
Painting the heavens grey
And blotting out the light
Leaving nothing but frozen rain
And lightning that promises to burn

She is the face people still see
The voice that people still hear
They find comfort in her old patterns
Even though in all her years
She never felt this real

She is something I will unpick
Stitch by stitch from this skin
Until she is scrubbed clean away
And you will finally see
The person I'm supposed to be

Dates and Dragons

Elouise Abby

THE FIRST TIME I told my mother I was leaving the house to go "role-play with my Dungeon Master" for an evening, I found myself a part of a very intense conversation about safe sex and the influences of modern literature. I tried to explain that, in fact, me and some friends were meeting up at their house for a tabletop game where we pretended to be fantasy characters and fight monsters. It wasn't until I busted out my collection of colourful, multi-sided dice that she realised I was telling the truth. This child would not be having intercourse that day.

Wednesdays are my favourite day of the week. Every Wednesday, my best friend hosts our weekly Dungeons and Dragons session. For three hours of an evening, we forget the lives we live day to day and become a rag-tag party of adventurers in a grand fantasy world. For half a decade, my group consisted of just the five of us. There was me, my best friend, Casey, who would run the games, her partner, Sean, his friend Nicholas, and a mutual friend Taylor. When we started out, I hadn't known Nicholas or Taylor that well. Even Sean was just my bestie's partner. Now, these four people were probably the closest friends I had in this world. We bonded over our game. Mishaps became inside jokes. We'd chat about our lives and what was going on, as well as theorise and scheme about what we'd end up doing in our next sessions. I guess seeing the same four people, three hours a week for five years will inevitably either endear you to them or drive you to commit murder. Someone had yet to be killed, so odds were looking good it was the former.

Last year, Nicholas landed his dream job in London, and we said goodbye to him. It was a bittersweet time. There were tears, and hugs, and promises to stay in touch. Before we knew it, life continued, and our little merry band of five became four. We eventually came to the conclusion that our games were lacking something, the stew of our weekly nerd-outs was missing an ingredient, so to speak. We decided to ask our friends and acquaintances if they knew anyone who might be interested in playing with us, and that's when Sean's uncle approached him.

"You still looking for someone to join your dragon club or whatsit called?"

"Yes," he said, presumably harnessing every ounce of self-restraint to refrain from adding, *"but actually..."*

"Our Lisa's niece just moved to the area. She likes all that pretend wizards rubbish. She's not got many friends local. Couldn't do us a favour and invite her to your thing, could you?"

And so it was that Jess came into my life.

We had heard Jess was a fan of Dungeons and Dragons too, apparently having played with her dad when she was young. She seemed like the perfect person to join the group now that Nicholas was gone. So, Casey invited her to join our next session.

***

If I could go back in time and talk to myself the day I had met her, I'd probably give myself this advice: *"Please close your mouth."*

There was me, late twenties, in a dirty hoodie stacking dice at a dining table, blissfully unaware of my sexuality, when in walks this woman...

Her bright turquoise side-cut, long and vibrant, drew me like a moth to a flame. I was instantly entranced. She was dressed in a black tank top and shorts with fishnets. A leather jacket was folded in her arms. There was a smell of sandalwood that seemed to follow her into the room.

All at once, I became aware of my messy hair, my dirty hoodie, and lack of bra. *Fuck!* DnD night hadn't required me to make an effort with my appearance in years, not since the gang had become so familiar with each other. The group's clothing priorities on a Wednesday had inevitably slid from style to comfort. It hadn't occurred to me that I was meeting someone new today.

"I love your top." She gestured to my faded Sailor Moon hoodie with a smile. "Sailor Moon was my favourite show as a kid."

The thing was about two sizes too big for me and had some dubious stains that I could honestly say I no longer remembered the origin of. It was also *extremely* comfortable, which was largely why I kept it around. Wearing it was like walking around in a socially acceptable blanket. "Thanks," I said, self-consciously brushing some stray hair behind my ear.

"Yeah, I loved it too. I bought this when I was younger, but I've lost some weight since then, so it kinda sits baggy. It's really comfortable though."

She nodded as I continued to ramble.

"Oh, but I'm a mess! Sorry you have to deal with me looking like this. I forgot I was meeting you tonight, or I would've tried harder."

She waved me off. "Nah, don't worry. You look ready to relax and play a game with friends. If I hadn't just come from town, I'd have opted for my safety hoodie too."

I laughed. Almost *too* instantly. Definitely too loudly. I slapped my hand to my face in a feeble attempt to stop further noise escaping. She smiled at me, and I felt my cheeks heat as all the blood in my body rose to my face. Thankfully, Sean chose that moment to return from a bathroom break, and the introductions that followed quickly brushed away the moment.

The evening went well. Jess told us a bit about herself, how she was new in town and had family here, how she'd just gone through a nasty break-up with her partner and wanted to start fresh. She was into heavy metal, obviously, and loved animals. We got on great and without really realising, I was discovering that as a woman, I could find another woman *extremely* attractive.

***

The next session rolled around, and Jess's character joined the crew. Her name was Roxha, and she was a half-orc, half-human warrior from a distant land.

"Roxha's a badass," she said. "Covered head to toe in tattoos and piercings. She's ripped and takes no crap from anyone."

I fanned my face in a mock gesture of demure arousal, which got a laugh from the table. "I'm Lucina," I said, introducing my fictional persona of nearly three years. "I was but a poor orphan girl, gifted with magic powers. I was adopted by a powerful wizard and taught to control my magic. Now I am a gallant adventurer, roaming the world helping people in need." I caught the hint of a wry smile on Jess's face.

"What kind of things do you like to do, Lucina?" she asked, voice low and gruff, in the style of a buff, orcish woman.

I hammed up my own accent, pronouncing each word with a laboured clarity. "Why, my dear, I am an avid lover of books. When I'm not fighting the forces of evil, I'll while away the time with a good story or non-fiction tome." I could hear the amused sighs of my friends as I mimed opening a big, dusty book and flicking through its pages.

"Okay," Jess said, dropping the character suddenly. "I've decided Roxha also finds nerds hot."

I froze. Jess was looking at me, smirk plastered on her face. I could hear my friends giggling.

"Watch out, Lucina!" Casey laughed.

I eventually joined in, chuckling as I looked towards her with a mock frown. When I turned back to Jess, she was still looking at me. I almost trembled under her gaze. Her eyes were a beautiful sea-foam green, iris gems nested in a sea of white, refusing to shy away as I stared.

"Everything okay?" Sean's voice came from the far opposite end of the table, snapping the pair of us back to reality.

"Yes," Jess said, her shoulders loosening as she turned to address the table once more.

I mimicked her, turned to the group, and nodded my confirmation that everything was indeed fine, but in my mind, I was a million miles away. Had Jess just eyed me up? Did she *like* me? Surely that couldn't be the case. She had just got out of a serious relationship. I didn't even know if she fancied women. I didn't even know if *I* fancied women.

***

Jess and I exchanged numbers, as she did with the rest of the group, so we could add her to our WhatsApp group for planning and sharing nerdy memes. Months passed, and we met every Wednesday for our weekly game. Jess quickly became embedded into our group.

The exchange between us on our second meeting wasn't the last time Jess and I had a *moment.* I would catch her looking at me, or we'd find ourselves smiling at each other for no clear reason. At one point, I reached past her to grab a pen, and my hand brushed against hers. My body bristled with a warm chill. It was like a spark of lightning shot through my every limb, and things started to make a lot of sense.

We would also chat, just the two of us. Share our opinions on music, TV, which animals were the cutest. You know, the usual stuff. We delved into some deeper topics too. Eventually, she told me about her ex, Alex.

Dates and Dragons

"Alex was the love of my life," Jess had said. "At least, I thought she was."

She? *She.* Until now, Jess had mentioned Alex only in passing. Like a fool, I had assumed the name to belong to a man, but this changed everything. Alex was a woman. Jess was a lesbian, or at the very least, bisexual.

Until Jess walked into my life, I'd never really thought much about relationships. I knew I wasn't interested in guys. Sure, I'd dated a few, but being with them romantically didn't appeal. I knew what asexuality was, and I'd assumed it applied to me.

It was a new and confusing feeling: wanting to be with someone. Wanting with every part of my being to impress them, to catch their attention wherever I could. Did she feel the same ? What if the flirting and the looks were just joking around? What if the excitement I felt when I touched her hand was just one-sided?

I decided they were questions I didn't want the answers to, and so I pushed the feelings to one side. Jess was a good friend, and I wouldn't want anything to ruin that.

***

"The dragon's talon clenches tight around you, Lucina, preventing any hope of escape. You feel the sharp, razor-like claw dig into your thigh, drawing the stinging warmth of blood. You are faint from your wounds, the edges of your vision blur and darken, threatening to seize your conscious mind."

We held our collective breath as Casey described the scene.

"Roxha. You stand before the dragon, your axe held tight within your sweat-slicked palms. It holds your friend Lucina within its mighty talon, ready to crush what life remains from her body. Around you, the rest of your companions lay still, slain by the beast. You are the last hope to lay the beast low and save the land from its reign of terror."

"I raise my axe," Jess says, "and plant it square in the skull of the beast!"

She grabs her dice from the table and shakes it. She kisses the back of her hand and whispers something to the polyhedral fates within. She releases it, and the dice clacks against the wood surface. It bounces and stops. And lands on a twenty.

The four of us roar with excitement.

Casey says, "You bring your axe down, blade first, into the head of the dragon and with a sickening crack, you penetrate its thick scales. The axe meets the soft, vulnerable matter of the dragon's brain, and its life is snuffed out in a mere instant. The talon around you goes limp, Lucina. You are free once more."

"I run over to her," Jess says, picking up immediately. "I hold her in my arms to support her as I know she's hurt, and I hold her tight. I couldn't save them," says Jess in her best Roxha voice. "I tried, I'm sorry. I'm so sorry...but you're still here."

We laugh, getting caught up in the moment.

"It's okay," I say, giving my Lucina an air of melodrama. "You did everything you could."

Without warning, Jess reaches across the table, grabbing my hand and holding it in hers. The air immediately leaves my lungs.

"I don't know what I would've done if I had lost you, Lucina. I've been a fool."

I watch Jess as she speaks, the lines between our game and reality beginning to blur.

"Since the day we first met, I've had feelings for you. The way you carry yourself with such majesty and skill. You are wise, and beautiful, and beyond compare. Amid a sky of stars, you shine ever the brightest in my eyes. I should have told you how I felt sooner. I don't know whether you feel the same but, having nearly lost you, I couldn't live with myself if I didn't tell you how I felt. I love you."

I sat there, hand in hers, for what felt like an entire lifetime. Her eyes remained locked on me, taking in every part of my reaction. I stared back at her, dumbfounded, until I felt the knobbly jab of Taylor's elbow in my side.

I quickly found myself again and picked up where she had left off. "Roxha," I say, "I love you too!"

"The two of you kiss, and it's the beginning of a beautiful relationship," Casey says softly.

There's a hidden challenge in her tone.

I close my eyes and lean forward.

Collecting the A's

Renee Fischer

MY MEMORY IS A forest, and the trails are all grown over. Searching out my past becomes a fight against myself. If I try to navigate that forest, I get easily lost, entangled in the vines of my thoughts, never quite finding what I was looking for when I first went looking. If there ever was a roadmap, it has long since been misplaced. I'm sure there are paths where I could find long-lost treasures, glimpses of joy, and love, and happiness, as many as there are snatches of despair and anguish hiding behind zealous brambles.

There are paths that are familiar to my feet, where I find my family, my friends, my passions. And then there are those where I take one single step onto uneven terrain. I blink and I'm there...

I'm eleven years old sitting in Mrs Wickham's English class. I haven't decided if I like her or not yet. My brother says she's a terrible teacher, but I'm not sure he always has great opinions and besides, she's always been friendly to me. I don't remember what the lesson is, those details are lost to the fog at the edge of the clearing. I'm sitting near the front of the classroom, close to the door on the right, and completely ignoring the girl sitting next to me. I'd much rather be sitting next to Olivia, who sits in the row behind us, but Mrs Wickham isn't the kind of teacher to let us choose our own seats, especially not when we've only just started big school.

I picture the future I want, a future where I'm happy, and grown up, and no longer have to listen to teachers I haven't made my mind up about. Where I'm living alone in a flat in some city I don't know yet. All alone. I'm happy on my own. I don't care about having a boyfriend or girlfriend or significant other to take up my space, and I certainly don't want any snot-nosed kids running about the place. I can't see them from where I'm standing, but I know there are pets in this flat with me, cuddly ones with soft fur and big hearts. My friends live close by so I can see them whenever I like, and we're our own little family, although I don't know to call it that yet. I picture my life in this flat, all alone, and am utterly content.

It is a small moment of bliss in an otherwise busy day, an otherwise busy life, a moment swiftly forgotten.

Until I go wandering in the forest and find myself drawn back to that picture time and time again. I see it many times over the years, smile, and shrug it off. I don't pay attention to the details anymore. I pay it no mind. I go on with my day, on with my life.

At eleven, I knew who I was and the life I wanted. Sixteen years later, I find myself faced with a fresh start and no idea where to begin. I've collected labels over the years, and none of them have led me to happiness.

I collected the first label at thirteen, when I called myself bisexual. Then I was a lesbian. Then a homoromantic bisexual. Then the magical day came when I found a new word, and a whole new world opened up.

Asexual.

Like many other depressed, queer teenagers and not-so-teenagers, I was on Tumblr. It was the second year of university, and I'm sitting in the lounge of the flat I share with Laura, a friend I will never speak to again after we both move out, as it happens, and my feet are up on the coffee table. In all probability, although I can't remember for certain, there's an empty sandwich box from a meal deal next to me and a crisp packet that's fallen to the floor. And there they are, in front of me, a stranger on the internet gifting me a word I didn't know I needed. A word that clicked as soon as I saw it. Oh, sure, there will be a late-night, alcohol-fuelled identity crisis to come and a stressful summer spent trying to figure out how to tell my then-girlfriend that I'm not who she thought I was when we started dating. (Eventually, we have a mutually agreed upon break-up when I come out to her, a recognition of us wanting different things, that leaves me with a silent, aching wound that tells me I'm not good enough for not being the person I advertised myself to be.)

The first A felt good. It felt right. It felt like maybe I actually could find that LGBT+ community that people always talked about. I had a way to explain why I got uncomfortable with kissing that got even slightly heated, not knowing where it would progress or how to say no to what might come next. I had a way to explain my aversion to overtly sexual club nights. I had a way to explain to potential partners that being physically intimate wasn't something I wanted; it wasn't anything to do with them, I just simply didn't experience that kind of attraction. (But don't worry, I still love you, I'm not entirely dysfunctional. You can work with that, right?)

The branches above me creak uneasily, urging me onto another path, another memory.

The next A wasn't an A for another four years. It showed up disguised as an NB and an afterthought, and the A wouldn't show up for a while yet. My friends were talking about gender, and names, and pronouns, and I sat back and watched, listened, and took it home and thought about it all. One evening before we went out to the pub, I sent a message to the group chat. *Call me Wren. Please don't call me a girl. I'm trying something out.*

I changed my name by deed poll and never looked back. I played with presentation, buying binders, button-up shirts, and men's jeans from Primark. And I enjoyed watching my curves disappear behind boxy shapes and practically sized pockets. I kept my hair short and enjoyed how it changed my face, how it felt, like I was looking at me in the mirror for the first time in my life. How was it possible to go twenty-two years without recognising yourself in the mirror?

The nonbinary stuck around and still does. Easy shorthand for the uninitiated, a quick way to explain that I am neither man nor woman but something outside of their perception. I am nothing, and I am filled with the freedom it gives me. The A? It came later. *Agender* finally pinned down my particular version of outside the binary, a way to explain what I would jokingly call gendervoid. Coming out as agender was unnecessary. The people important to me knew I was nonbinary already. They used the right name for me, they knew I was neither this nor that–it was close enough. It was an A that I was happy to share but one I kept quiet.

Another twisty, shadowed path through the forest. A trail that leads to a place I don't want to revisit. Sunlight shines through the leaves, and I follow it eagerly, seeking out the warmth on my cheeks. I'm blinded by that light, not noticing the roots reaching for my heels.

I found a partner who said she was asexual too. We went through thick and thin together. We shared our hopes and dreams for the future. I supported her as she started her transition. She supported me as I dropped out of university and wrangled with trying to find self-worth outside of my parents' expectations for my future. We were happy.

I was meant to have a love story, the world told me. This was mine, and I wasn't going to let it go.

I proposed to her under a gazebo in a stately garden, a moment of privacy for just us. A rough diamond on a necklace for her, and a ring we would choose together later for me. Years later, she lost the necklace, and she still hadn't paid me back for my ring. I let it slide, as I let anything that threatened my relationship slide. Like all those niggling questions at the back of my head, the doubts that kept me awake when she said she wasn't asexual after all, and actually she did want sex, and could we work towards it? The little voice that asked me, what did love feel like anyway? Was this love? How were you supposed to know? We built a life together and that was enough. It had to be.

I thought our foundations were stable. I thought we were unshakeable. I thought a lot of things.

Most of them were wrong.

The vines snatch at me, pulling me in, and suddenly I'm tangled and trapped. I know this memory; it's fresh, and painful, and the thorns warn me to turn back. They tell me not to get too close. It will only hurt. But I can see it right there in front of me, and they hold me hostage, forcing me to confront myself. Glimpses come through in the gaps between the leaves, and I know I can only wander the safe paths for so long.

I'm grieving my dad who died months ago, a new wound to carry with me, this one open, and gaping, and causing severe blood loss. I'm struggling to find my feet and then...

The third A.

The third A isn't easy, or joyful, or simple. Nothing about it clicks. Nothing about it makes me feel proud of my identity. It's a word I can say easily until it comes to my own identity, and then it gets stuck in my throat.

I wonder if there's another clearing on the other side of this thicket. If only I can be brave enough to fight my way through to it, maybe I could lay in the grass and let the sun warm my skin as it heals the scratches from the clinging thorns. The pain of change.

It's the question I've been too scared to ask. I'm trying to find my footing again on the blood-soaked ground that gives way beneath my scrambling bare feet. Maybe asking the question will be the tremor that brings down the mudslide.

Maybe the mudslide is coming anyway. Maybe it's inevitable.

(I was meant to have a love story, the world told me. Where did I go wrong?)

The old ache of *not good enough* twinges deep inside my chest, bringing back Maddy's face when we parted ways, neither meaning to cause hurt but carrying it for years anyway. It never went away, not really; it's right here, ready to break open again and show people my deep, dark truth, the one hidden at the centre of this overgrown maze.

I'm not who I said I am. I don't come as advertised. You bought into this relationship under false pretences.

If I tell you the third A I've collected, nothing will be as I pictured it. We won't grow old together, surrounded by cats, a family of just us two, us against the world.

I'll be alone.

I've not been alone in so long. You've been by my side for six years, and the time before that is lost to the weeds now. I'm not sure I could find my way back there. I don't want to. But I can't find my way forward either.

Even as it all comes to an end, I can't say the third A. We both know it's there, hanging in the space between us, as I curl up on the floor next to the beige sofa and cling onto your hand, shaking and crying in fear that *this*, this will break me.

The change is happening around me, the mudslide gaining speed, and I still can't say the damn word out of fear of what it will bring.

I sit in the kitchen of my friend's house, cup of tea in hand, bags of hastily packed clothes on the floor beside me, and ask them how they know. How can they know what is platonic and what is romantic? Can they define it? Or put it into a simple tick-box definition I can hold onto when nothing else makes sense? I dance around the third A, and they know–*of course they know*–but they don't make me say it.

They offer me a bedroom, guinea pigs to cuddle, and open hearts. I begin to rebuild.

I break through to the clearing and lie in the grass. The cherished ring, with its tiny diamonds like flowers, is lost in the mud behind me. It will never be the same again.

I lie there for a long time. The sun sets. Rain comes and washes the mud from my wounds. I can smell the damp leaves beneath me, the sweet scent of new growth getting stronger. The scrapes from the thorns close up, and new skin takes their place, pink and sensitive. The scabs are gone, but the vulnerability remains.

I look across the path and see me at eleven: long hair and pleated navy school skirt, picturing the future. When did this moment become lost to the fog and the weeds? How did we end up on such different paths, she and I?

It doesn't look anything like how I'd pictured it. There are far more crocheting and video games involved, but the bones are there. I live alone, I have plans to get pets when the landlord signs off on it, my friends are the family I've dreamed of, and they're only a stone's throw away. I'm alone, and I'm happy.

The love story I needed wasn't one with a diamond ring, and a white dress, and a happily ever after.

The love story was me. Me and all three of my As.

Asexual.

Agender.

Aromantic.

I walk out of my forest with my head held high and the mists at my back, striding forward to new paths unseen. I will make new memories in a forest full of sunshine.

Declaration of Love

Vanessa Ball

Saturday 9th July 2022

HAVE I TOLD YOU how much I love you recently? No? Well, let me remind you. I love you for all your quirks and differences. For all the struggles and challenges you've overcome in your life. For all the strength you've had to muster and show the world. For all the secrets you've finally unearthed and put on the table for all to bear witness to. I love you.

It was never going to be an easy ride for you, my sweet child. You, with a heart so full of love and no safe place to call home. You wandered alone for so long, with all the questions and no clear answers.

What a lonely place you found yourself in. But that was the answer all along: you. To find yourself. To live yourself. And knowing that people will come and go, some with good intent, others blinded by their own pain and inner struggles, But you, child, will always be the constant in your life.

To ask yourself, with love and grace, what do you want in this life? Do you always want to be true to yourself? Is it important that you never have to live with the weight of a lie hanging around your neck? Causing you to always look down with shame rather than up at the beauty that exists all around.

Do you want to always live in fear of what others may think of you because of their own misguided beliefs? Or do you want to speak your truth and know that there are many who have come before you? Who have lived through their own personal battles and are here, ready to embrace you for who you truly are and what you stand for: love and acceptance for all.

The fear you once knew held you back, created barriers between you and your happiness. But there are those around who would happily share in that happiness, nurture it, and watch it blossom.

So I ask you, dear child, all too cautious of everyone and everything. Let down your guard, and walk freely into the beautiful present that accepts you for all you are and always have been.

A child of love.

Humpback Whales

Saffron Sage

You say, let's go swim with the whales.
I laugh and tell you that will never happen.
I don't like deep water, and I have a fear of sharks.
You tell me whatever is meant to be will happen.
You make it happen by booking a trip.
You go diving and see no whales.
I go snorkelling and see no whales.
On the boat, you see whales at a distance, but we can't keep up.
We get put in the water near a whale, and it takes off, and we don't see it.
I freak out in the deep water, and you stay with me to keep me calm.
I didn't want to get back in the water, and you told me you wouldn't leave me. I trust you.
We get back in the water. There are no depths I won't dive with you.
There! A mummy whale with her baby float gracefully side by side.
I squeal with delight through my snorkel. Bubbles rise.
I am suspended in their world. Time stops.
Mummy whale stares right back at us with her wise, deep-seeing eye.
Baby curiously watches us too.
A spiritual, emotional connection is forged there in the deep.
Such a wise, graceful life force, and she trusted us for a few minutes there in the sea, where we were interlopers.
One powerful rock of her tail, and we were left in her wake. They were gone.
Every time I closed my eyes for weeks after, I could feel the ocean carrying me, see her gentle gaze, sense the power.
I can still see the awe in your expression that mirrored my own feelings.
You got me to dive in, and it changed me.
You made one of my dreams come true. You seem to do that a lot.
Even now, we both smile when we see humpback whales on TV. It was our special moment, our time in the deep.

Saffron Sage

You and I have this amazing spiritual connection, and you've made me embrace my lesbian self and to nurture her.
There are no dreams that are not unobtainable if you're in my life as my lesbian fellow warrior and protector.

Lost and Found

Hazel Clark

It Begins

OH, FOR GOODNESS SAKE. There I was again, fighting with one of the shackles. It was a really hot day, which didn't help my irritability level with a rigging issue. I sighed and looked up at the sail with its comet logo proudly displayed along with the number, 685. It's a small dinghy with a once beautiful blue hull. It's still beautiful but with a slightly duller, used hull and a fair few scratches and bumps from my many races.

I wouldn't be sailing if I couldn't get this shackle attached. Honestly, it happens all the time. Every time I go to rig my dinghy sailing boat, I always seem to have that little bit of a disaster. It didn't help that my heart was already thumping. It was the start of the sailing season, and I was full of nerves. I don't know what it is that makes me so nervous. Is it the fact that I'm starting from scratch again? No series done, no races done, no trophy days done; I'm literally starting over. Or is it that I haven't got on a boat for a couple of months because it's been winter? I'm not sure if it's that either. It's a bit like riding a bike, really. When you've done it once, no matter how long the gap, you can still remember how to do it.

I've been sailing for three years. At thirty-six, I should've been sailing longer, but life had been full of football until I'd had to stop playing. I still need to scratch that competitive itch though, so I'd taken up sailing. Yes, it was a little bit late, but I was finding my feet. And, oh, the nerves that got me. Always worse at the start of the season, and even more so if it was a bit windy, but today the wind was fine, so I was feeling good.

"Oh, come here."

Ah, there she is. Whenever I get myself a bit stuck, or whenever my heart pounds too much, or whenever I get too nervous, there's always Joe, calming as ever. Here I am, flapping about and overthinking. Whenever I have something to worry about, she says the same thing. "It will be all right. Don't worry about it."

I'm an overthinker. I mean, if I can't get my sail up, I can't get on the water on time, and then I'm going to get all flustered and fall in. Joe? She's just, "Yeah, don't worry about it. Give it here, I'll fix it." That's Joe all over.

You can see why I nicknamed her Superhero. I let myself drift into memories of us together. Initially, her nickname originated from a pair of pyjamas that had superheroes running towards you, the question "Did someone call for a superhero?" emblazoned around them.

Let's be honest, the pyjamas were only a small part of why I called her Superhero. She really had been my hero.

I was one of life's quirky people and had been subjected to severe bullying in my earlier years. People leave school with qualifications, memories, and friends. I'd left with qualifications, yes, but also with a fear of rejection, judgement, failure, and hurt. I'd locked myself away from the potential of falling in love because it didn't feel safe enough. Judgement, rejection, and vulnerability were all things I had massively avoided, but Joe had come and squashed all those worries like a giant squashes a pea. I just didn't have those worries anymore, well, not with her anyway. Yes, she'd definitely earned her Superhero moniker for way more than just a pair of pyjamas.

Honestly, I have no idea how I managed to get with Joe or how she even got into this situation at all. It was always going to have to be someone special to break down my walls, and she was *very* special. Why she ever looked my way, I will never know. She didn't even like sailing, and yet here she was, cheering me on. She was there because she knew how much it meant to me. She plays football, and I watch her, but I *like* football! And I coach it too. It's how we met.

My pondering of the past stopped when she looked at me.

"Done it," she said, and I moved closer to take the shackle from her. "Ah, ah" she said, tapping her cheek and giving me one of those mischievous grins of hers.

"Oh, you want a prize?" I asked confidently, though I felt anything but confident. Everyone else was rigging their boats up. Was anyone looking in my direction? I wanted so badly to kiss her and thank her for her marvellous work, but would anyone say anything? I looked over at Joe. Wasn't it obvious anyway? I mean, Dad always joked she looked like the famous cartoon lesbian Millie Tant. I kissed her cheek. Did anyone notice? I don't think so, but if they did, they didn't say anything. As I set out onto the water, I looked back at her. Why was I so concerned about what people thought? She is literally my world, my rock, my home, and my safe space. So did it matter? Surely it didn't?

If anyone with a man felt like this, then they'd be shouting it from the rooftops. Me? I'm worried, because my partner is the same gender as me. Sounds ridiculous when you write it like that. Yet I knew as soon as I started to tell people, it wouldn't seem like a ridiculous issue at all. But when you're from a religious background in a time when being gay has only just started to be talked about, it does make a difference. Forty years ago was the eighties, and AIDS was linked with being gay. So maybe my concerns weren't unfounded. Who was to say things had progressed much since then? I was soon about to find out just how valid my concerns were.

Conflict

I saw my nannie every single week. She would always get the teapot out and make me a cup of tea. She would fuss about what milk I used. Did I have my tea bags? Did I want a biscuit? We discussed church, sailing, and other family news while we sat in the conservatory looking over the small garden. Nannie was always one to keep the conversation going and always had something to worry about. Had Dad got the shopping list she sent? Had Dad taken the tomato plant out of the car? What time were we meeting at such and such a place? You get the idea. Nannie loved me unconditionally and spoke about me with such pride. It sounds perfect, and it very much was. I had my family, and my faith, and a new girlfriend, and they were the three most important things in my world.

However, I actually felt like I was living a parallel life. While I was seeing my grandparents, I was selecting what to tell them, hiding my phone (because Joe was on my wallpaper), and monitoring everything I said. I was scared to show a photo on my phone in case Joe text at the same time, and they saw the notification.

Then my dad dropped the bombshell. Joe wasn't my friend–she was my girlfriend. I'd always said to him that if the conversation headed in that direction at any point, then to tell them. It was going to have to come out at some point anyway. I had a very special relationship with my dad, and he always said he would tell them to rescue me. It's the uncertainty of not knowing what they might say or the quickness in which I'd have to answer what they threw at me that worried me. Under conflict, I shut down and I can't always find the words I need. My relationship with Joe wasn't going to go away, and as we became more entangled in each other's lives, it was becoming harder for me to live two separate ones, one with Joe and one without. To be honest, I was relieved when I found out Dad had told them that Joe was my partner. I wouldn't have wanted him to lie when Nannie was talking to him about hoping I found someone special one day. Joe *was* my special someone. She was my partner and was rapidly becoming my whole world.

The next time I went to see them, it was like nothing had happened.

Nannie spent the whole time asking about all aspects of my life apart from Joe, while she constantly offered me biscuits and drinks. We were avoiding the biggest part of my life. I didn't bring it up either to start with. I was too scared to, because I wasn't very good at thinking on my feet, and my heart pounded when I was under criticism and pressure. I got used to it. Yes, it hurt, but I got used to it. I got used to hearing how she'd visited her other grandchildren in their houses, how she was proud of their marriages and their children. I even took the hit of hurt when seeing pictures of happy family outings and realised that I was never going to see pictures of me and Joe doing things with my grandparents. They had been very clear with my dad that they wouldn't have Joe in the house or attend my events where she was present because they didn't "want to be seen to encourage it." In response, my dad said, "We don't want to be seen to encourage homophobia." My parents had my back, and that definitely reduced the pain I felt, because they were actively encouraging me to be with whoever I wanted to be with and to be happy.

Eventually, it came up in conversation. It was unavoidable in the long run.

"I haven't told anyone," she said. "Coming out isn't something we do here."

I didn't know what to say to that... Well, I did but I couldn't say it. I wanted to go on a rant about the need for people like me to have to say something, because I knew they wouldn't agree with it, so it was going to be a big deal. However, I didn't want to start with that. I had no battle in me, so I didn't say anything at all. I just sat there. Sometimes, I wanted to scream at myself to speak up and stand up for my relationship, but I couldn't face it. However, as the weeks went by, it came up more often and not in a good way, and not just with me either.

"I don't understand. They're identical twins and had the same upbringing, so how come one of them is okay and the other isn't?"

Okay to them meant being married to a Christian man, living in a nice house, and having a family. Nannie also decided to tell me that she would never come to my wedding if I married a woman. That certainly made me want to scream inside. Where's the logic in that? You aren't coming to my wedding not because she's a mass murderer, a horrible person, committed a crime, or robbed a bank, but because she's a woman. Outside, I pretended it was fine. I told them I would send them an invite if it happened, but if they didn't come, that was their choice. I wouldn't want someone at my wedding who didn't support my union. Fair enough, I get it. You see it as a sin, but don't then go to another grandchild's wedding who has been living in sin by having pre-marital sex. The sins are rated and cherry-picked. Logically, it made no sense. When I challenged her this way, I was told it was because "the sin is different."

One day, me and Nannie went to Sainsbury's. It was hot, so hot that even touching the trolley handle could get you third-degree burns. I'd found some new confidence since meeting Joe and was enjoying being able to wear my favourite shorts away from the house, along with my sunglasses. Instead of seeing my body as something to hide, along with the rest of me, I started to see myself as okay, and that was a massive leap. Nannie was in her usual dress and sandals which made that clip clop sound. As we walked into the shop, we were hit by a welcome blast of cold air from the air con. We had just walked past an electric car charging station, so I was chatting away about how I wanted to get one to save money, and I'd get a house with a drive so I could have an electric port fitted.

"You don't need to be buying a house yet. You've got years for that."

Bear in mind, I'm thirty-five and well beyond the age for living at home. I waited for her to go on as I could tell she had something more to say.

"I don't think you're gay."

I wasn't going to start this conversation in the doorway of a supermarket. I didn't want to have that conversation at all, in fact. "Let's not start this again," I said.

Then Nannie started talking again about how it had been such a shock and how it had impacted her. It was all a bit vague and to be honest, I tried to switch off. Not because I didn't care but because I cared too much, and

I knew it would end with me either crying or getting very angry.

"I can still love you and not love the woman who took away our lovely Hazel." She clip-clopped ahead of me.

Oh, dear. She'd pressed the button. "I don't think I am in any way less lovely." My head started spinning, and I could feel myself getting more and more wound up. Here I was being judged constantly for being gay, something which Jesus himself never discussed. He told us to love everyone. I wanted to start a massive rant, but the noise of the supermarket hit me. People chatting, the tills being open and shut, and the sound of trolleys being pulled along the floor. *Not now, Hazel, not now.*

"Look, let's get a coffee. I get twenty percent off with my Blue Light card." I worked for the NHS and was proud of it.

"Yes, let's get lunch first before we do the shopping," Nannie replied, seemingly unaware that I was close to breaking something.

We walked into the café. They did an array of vegan sandwiches and wraps, and they also had vegan whipped cream for all those posh drinks. I turned to the left to look in the fridge cabinet. I tried to focus on the choices and look for the green label, but my heart was pounding, and my stomach no longer wanted to accept the wonderful food I'd been thinking about since I woke up this morning.

"I don't know which option to have," I mumbled. The sick feeling was now in my throat.

Nannie chose something we could share but then changed her mind when she saw a teacake. "We're women. We're allowed to change our minds," she said. "Something that feels so right now can change in the future."

She mentioned Joe's name, but I'd done that thing where I switch off when under attack. I needed to give her a response, but my annoyance was hard to control. "Be prepared that some things don't change either." With that, I went to get the drinks from the collection point before I completely lost it, while Nannie went and sat down. When I joined her, she started chatting about food and shopping, and neither the conversation at the front of the supermarket or at the counter was mentioned, like it had never happened.

I couldn't pretend it hadn't happened. I sat there wondering how someone who had known me from birth and held me as a child could suddenly change the unconditional love ethos of our family. Or maybe it had always come with conditions, and I simply hadn't been aware of them until I didn't do what was expected of me. Nannie's wasn't the only relationship that came with expectations of what and who I should be.

***

I threw my phone across the room, and it hit the sofa with a soft bump. "I'm not even bothering to answer to that." In truth, I wanted to answer it. But the anger pounding in my chest and the lump in my throat told me it would be a bad idea. Twelve years meant nothing. Our growth together through early adulthood, watching her get married and have her child, going on holiday together, staying with her family, doing charity work together, breaking the language barrier and learning her culture in Bulgaria, endless late nights playing *Ticket to Ride*, discussing God and life, sharing our faith, sharing the many different flavoured fruit juices (I'll never forget the cactus juice), and the endless ice creams... None of our past seemed to matter. Our friendship was over.

Did I regret telling Krasi about Joe? I didn't feel I had any choice. She was weeks away from coming to England from Bulgaria, her home, and staying on the next street to me in an Airbnb. What was I supposed to do? Hide my girlfriend in the hope she didn't bump into us both? Or maybe I should take the photos down of us in the house when she visited? But what about the dressing gown and slippers, or the fact that my phone might ring while we were together? Should I pretend we were just friends? But then I wouldn't be able to say "I love you" at the end of a call. Always saying I love you before departing from my superhero had become an important part of our relationship. Why should I sacrifice that because Joe was a woman? I'm not harming anyone. Why am I hiding my life like I'm committing a crime? I'm in love, not committing murder.

So I decided to tell her. I wasn't shocked by her response, but I was shocked by the sheer number of messages and the nature of them in the month after. They were full of judgement about my relationship. I went through the grieving process and watched our twelve-year friendship slowly disintegrate. I felt every emotion as if someone had died, which in a way, someone had. The image of the person she thought I was had departed. She didn't wish me well, in a series of texts, either:

I honestly think it is better for you to be alone in this life than the eventual possibility of spending eternity in hell.

I don't feel you need to fill the place of a husband with a woman.

I'm sure this is not God's plan for you...and I definitely know whose plan for you this is...the plan of the enemy of your soul. The one who doesn't want you in heaven.

The way I see it is that you are headed to the edge of a cliff and going to jump...and you think you can fly and I know that you can't.

Why do you think God made you this way? He didn't make people drug-addicted or murders.

People who say they accept this, they don't care for you...they just care for themselves, because confrontation is hard and they don't want to go through it.

Your mind is very tricked, but this can be fixed as long as you start thinking the right thoughts.

She made it very clear that I couldn't live the life of a Christian woman and date a woman.

Krasi wasn't the only one who didn't think I could be a Christian and be gay. My church clearly stated that they saw marriage as between a man and a woman. Honestly, I didn't even have the energy to fight, so I just quietly slipped away under the guise that I had too much going on in my life. In my hunt for a new church, I found one which accepted gay Christians, and the curate was even married to another woman.

However, it was thirty minutes away, and the style of worship was very different to what I knew. It didn't quite fit, like a jacket just a little too tight. I tried another one in the city centre and went for several weeks. The worship was more my style, and the sermons were discussing real life issues including relationship breakups and divorce. But about three weeks in, the pastor of the church stated in his sermon that "gender and sexuality was moving more away from God." He never discussed or even backed his statement up. It was even more infuriating that this was in the middle of a sermon in which he was discussing the church's inclusivity. At that point, I just gave up looking.

Church and being a Christian had always been part of who I was. I always identified as a Christian, so why couldn't I find a church? I felt lost and confused. I was still a child of God, right? I mean, God didn't hate me...did he? I continued to read my Bible every night and pray. I noticed my concentration slip, and I resorted to reading a Bible verse a day and small passages rather than a longer reading. I found myself writing prayers to stay focused and looking for hope that everything would be all right.

Then one evening, my mum showed me a church she'd found online. "We welcome those who are single, happily married, unhappily married, divorced, gay, or desperate. We welcome those who are tattooed, pierced, or cut. We offer a special welcome to those who have been Bible-bashed, had religion shoved down their throat as a kid, or have been let down by the church." Well, that was bold advertising. It looked good, but I was just too done to want to try again. What I didn't realise was that Mum had already messaged them on my behalf.

"I have a gay daughter," she told them. "She's looking for a church where she can be accepted."

Their response stated they would welcome me but, "We would desire and encourage a change of lifestyle." The inclusivity this church pretended to have was actually just a shallow top layer with no substance underneath. How was that response anywhere near what they advised? They were Bible-bashing! Hardly a "special welcome."

Resolution

I'd met the love of my life and had become the happiest and most comfortable I had ever been, only to find that I'd also fallen off a cliff into a world of intolerance. I couldn't understand why the people I loved didn't share my happiness about me finding the person I wanted to spend my life with, the person who loved me for me and made me so happy. When my twin found her soulmate, there had been this massive party, congratulations, and love. For me, not so much. Nothing felt right about the judgement and rejection I was experiencing from people in the name of God. Where was the loving and inclusive nature of Jesus portrayed in the gospels and his main message all about love? Yes, my relationships with my family and friends were difficult, but the biggest obstacle to total contentment revolved around my faith.

I was being rejected by the religion I had followed all my life just by being me. I thought God loved me for being me, so why was I being rejected? How could God, who made me "in my mother's womb" (Psalm 139) then throw me out for being me? Did He now reject me because of my love and sexuality as the church and its followers seem to imply?

It was at that point I realised the truth. *God* was not rejecting me.

He made me this way. He talked about love. He healed the sick, He connected with outcasts, and He never rejected anyone. It was the church and people who rejected me under the disguise of God. If God cared so much about same-sex relationships, then why did Jesus never discuss it when he came to Earth? Not one of the seven verses from over forty-one thousand came from Christ himself. He *never* dealt with this issue. He *never* mentioned it. Most of the anti-gay messages come from St. Paul. This same Paul also condemned men who wore clothes of more than one weave and women who didn't cover their heads in church. He also encouraged slaves to be good to their masters. Much of this has subsequently been dismissed as of the time or cultural. However, the anti-gay message seems to have remained unchallenged over the years, and if anything, it has been reinforced.

In a time when being married was important for property and populating the planet, it raises the question whether these messages are also of their time, like the others. Furthermore, there is the issue of the context in which gay relationships are written. They are all written about negatively. Even heterosexual relationships would be considered bad in these negative circumstances and situations. Additionally, there's the issue of interpretation. One Bible verse commonly quoted is, "Man should not lie with man." This has now been determined as an issue of interpretation. It's actually "man should not lie with boy." It's about paedophilia and not same-sex relationships. It's things like this, to do with interpretation and people discriminating against others, that has so impacted my journey, along with plenty of other people's.

The fact I managed to find a few churches who did support and encourage the LGBTQ+ community and also saw the Methodist Church legalise the marriage of same-sex relationships shows it is far from clear-cut. What sends me into a rage is the number of people who have been driven out by churches pretending to be inclusive when they aren't. My story is one of many. I'm not the only one whose faith has been challenged. But I'm happy to say that once I realized the messages I was getting were nothing more than human prejudice and had nothing to do with God's love, I found my faith once again.

Finding all of this out was massive for me. It allows me to be a Christian and be gay. I don't have to choose between them. It allows me to continue to have a relationship with God and be at peace with myself in the way

He created me. Finding other like-minded Christians helped, and there *are* churches out there who really are inclusive. Best of all, by actually opening up to people, I've had some great discussions and found a few like-minded people within my past who have been very supportive. Two influential people in my journey to this realisation were Matthew Vines, who wrote *God and the Gay Christian*, and the Naked Pastor, whose pictures really capture the loving nature of Jesus to people of the LGBTQ+ community.

I've also learned that you can't be responsible for other people's feelings. God wants us to love other people as we love ourselves. I really hope there may come a day where I travel to Bulgaria to see Krasi and do my charity work. I hope a day comes when I can knock on my grandparents' door like I used to, with Joe by my side. I hope there's a day in the world when any gay person can enter a church and be fully accepted as a child of God and accepted for who God made them. A day has to come, surely, where people don't use God to persecute people.

I haven't changed. I'm still me. I'm still Hazel. I'm being me, and my sexuality is just a tiny part of who I am. God made me who I am. Long story short, love you for being you just as God does. *Don't* lose your faith just because others are compelled to tell you how God sees your life. They're no more in touch with God than you. Live the best Christian life you can, follow the two most important commandments, which are love the Lord your God with all your heart, soul, and mind and love your neighbour as yourself. Remember, the Bible was written of its time. Being gay was never in the gospel. Jesus cured the sick and loved everyone, no matter what. He preached about love and inclusivity. People shouting at me and rejecting me for a biblical point, which has nothing to do with Christ himself, is ludicrous. Remember He made you *you*. Most importantly, remember "We love because God first loved us," so how can loving anyone be a crime? Love is a gift from God; it's a blessing and far more important than the gender of the person you are with.

As for Nannie and Grandpa, I still visit them every week for coffee. I still take Nannie out for shopping, and I wander around the garden to look at her flowers and plants. But it's different, there's no doubt about it. Nannie said she thought our relationship would stay the same. Dad questioned how it could, given the rejection I've experienced in the last year. Does she still mention it? Every other visit usually has a moment of her telling me how she doesn't agree with it. However, I'm lucky that my parents took a strong stand, and we're all in agreement that if Joe isn't invited to the big events, then none of us attend. And that's exactly what happened at my birthday. They wanted to see me in the afternoon with my twin, but they took away that invitation when they knew Joe was spending the day with me. In return, I didn't celebrate my birthday with them. It was their loss. I had a wonderful day.

Of course, I hope there will be a day when she comes to accept it and Joe can come round with me. For now, I have to kind of accept that she doesn't want that. She doesn't want Joe to be part of her family, and she doesn't have to. But she can't stop me from living my life or being with the only person I've ever been in love with: my superhero. She has her viewpoint, and I have mine. I must respect that. Does it hurt sometimes? Yes, of course it does. And it's usually when I think I've come fully to terms with it that something will happen, like my birthday. But yes, there has been movement. I can mention things now which I've done with Joe, like camping. Nannie either doesn't answer or talks about the size of the tent rather than any person in it, but it's progress.

I accept this is how it is right now, and maybe that's all the ending I actually needed. I found the love of my life, came to understand my faith and God in a different way, and I love how life is right now. I live in a world where not all Christians accept same-sex relationships. It's changing, though, and recently, some churches have begun to accept and authorise gay marriages. I am in a powerful place where I can help this change and where being gay doesn't mean you have to lose your faith or relationship with God. I need to shout louder than the persecution so we don't reject and lose other Christians who don't feel welcome. The alternative viewpoint needs to be heard. Like I said, God is love. And that has always been His main message.

Hindsight is a Wonderful Thing

Jamie Mann

JOSEPH PLAYED WITH THE idea of being an actor. Then he decided he was going to be an actor, no matter what. That was his resolution at seventeen.

Long before the reality of personal computers, internet, social media and mobile phones, boredom could strike at any time. Cinema and television were an obsessive ritual for Joseph, where his imagination could escape. Black and white films from his parents' era had become a fascination. On Sunday afternoons, he absorbed the films of Hollywood actresses like Joan Crawford or Bette Davis, finding he identified with the tough women who could handle themselves with quick-witted puns, shoot a gun, and get their man by the end of the movie. His instinct was to also find himself a man one day.

With Joseph's family being market gardeners, growing up had offered a great time outdoors. Acres of crops, orchards, a large home, and outbuildings offered plenty of space to explore his childhood imagination.

Ever since he could recall, Joseph knew that he felt somehow different from other boys. While affection and attraction for his own sex was always there, niggling away into his subconscious, he remained a typical boy. Building dens and acting out war games with a couple of close friends. When he reached his teens, he started to spend more time alone as an awareness of such feelings blossomed. Instinct told him to keep those feelings of male attraction to himself. Somehow, he was certain that such awkward emotions would go away, that the crushes he had started to feel for boys would refocus on girls. Eventually.

On leaving school, he began to help his parents. An older brother and sister in their twenties had long moved away to university and gave no indication of wanting to return to the family business. One day, Joseph would take over from his father, or so they believed. Yet a private ambition had bubbled through him from the age of fifteen. That ambition kept returning–to be someone else. Joseph could at least pretend to be other people, even if he couldn't change himself.

Taking solo trips to the cinema and watching every sci-fi television series possible, the idea of acting obsessed him. He learned that those people on silver screens were career actors. He imagined himself as Star Trek and then Star Wars characters. Joseph could be the action hero, wielding ray guns, fighting every alien possible. Unlike the men who got the girl in the end, Joseph always imagined getting a man.

His parents long considered Joseph's life mapped out. He would find a girl, marry, settle down in the village, and give them grandchildren. A couple of times, Joseph had invited a local girl home because he felt that was expected.

After such a visit, his mother would get very excited. "Joseph, she's lovely. When are you bringing her again?"

After school's end, a wedding of an older cousin took place that summer. Animated by their invitation, his mother became obsessed by the possibility of the family extension. "Joseph, why don't you bring Angela along?"

Joseph did as his mother bid. The day was more nerve-racking for him than the happy couple. Yet, he played it out. He danced with Angela, led her around by the hand, got her drinks, stood close to her, and talked endlessly. At moments, Angela gazed at Joseph, commenting on the cut of his dark blond hair and the colour of his eyes, clearly in expectation he would kiss her. But Joseph made no move to do so, except for a soft touch on the cheek at the end of the night. She stood outside her door with an expression of puzzlement when he simply waved and left.

Guilt and exhilaration filled Joseph as he played the role of a "normal" man. Throughout school he had taken every chance to take a role in any school play. A nativity shepherd, chimney sweep in Mary Poppins, and a pickpocket in Oliver Twist had all given him such a buzz. He didn't have to be normal when he was acting. That's when he felt most himself.

That was when he took the decision to take it to the next level. He applied for the one-year drama O-level course at the town's local technical college. Without telling anyone, Joseph attended an interview and short audition. He was asked to interpret the 'St Crispin's Day' Shakespeare speech from Henry V. He ran with it, recalling how at school the drama teacher had guided him on how to interpret and use inflection and emphasis on certain lines.

"He that shall live this day, and see old age, Will yearly on the vigil feast his neighbours, And say 'To-morrow is Saint Crispian.' Then will he strip his sleeve and show his scars, And say 'These wounds I had on Crispin's day.'"

The college drama tutor, Mr Phillips, was a strange, mature man who, possibly having come to a halt in his career of theatre-acting, drifted into teaching. He was sharp-eyed and prone to interrupting a student if they hesitated.

Despite nerves, Joseph focused on the interviewer, keenly answered questions about taking part in school plays and how he planned to go on to Rada in a year or two. All his anxieties stalled as he observed that Mr Phillips wore a hairpiece. Silent humour rubbed the back of his eyes. The toupee was badly fitting. Unconsciously, Mr Phillips occasionally pressed the hairpiece to his crown, making a scrunching noise as it stuck back to his scalp.

A few weeks later, Joseph's excitement at gaining a place on the course was tempered by informing his parents. Their initial reaction was of puzzled disappointment.

"Really?" said Dad, having never had a clue that his son wanted to be an actor. "That's not going to earn you any money, is it? I have to turn on the water." His father's displeasure was emphasised as he abruptly left the breakfast table.

After a minute, his mother put a hand on his. "You know what your father's like. He's not a great one for expressing himself, but you've always had a sensitivity."

"Look, Mum, I want to do this. I want to see if I can be any good at acting. Take it far as I can."

She squeezed his fingers. "That's okay, dear."

Despite her words, he could tell she was siding with Dad.

Relenting slightly, Joseph shrugged. "It might not work out. I might hate it. I don't know till I try. Perhaps I'll end up being a market gardener."

"Joseph." A spark of hope flickered into her eyes. "Do what you need to do."

"I've decided on Joe now. Call me Joe." He was already working on a stage name, feeling that Joseph Wasson was clumsy and lacked star quality. Maybe Joe Bond or Joe Flint.

Summer passed slowly. Joe avoided boredom by helping his dad. Harvesting crops and getting produce to local shops, restaurants, and markets. Neither mentioned his starting college in September. His dad appeared to have forgotten the idea, or perhaps believed his youngest son would get over the idea of drama school. Although he had rarely helped his mother on the market stand, Joe began to help twice a week, thinking he might increase his confidence by interacting with customers.

Joe idly observed their fellow market-sellers as they called out to potential buyers. After a week, Joe asked his mother what she thought about him having a go at pitching. As they were into the last couple of hours of the day, she told him to go for it. He attempted the technique as his mother returned with mugs of tea. At first, his words were clumsy. Joe blustered, choking out items for sale. After a few sips of tea, he tried again, working on the role. With relaxed shoulders, he breathed deeper. This time it worked. He found himself somehow taking on an East End accent.

"Get your strawberries here, lovely lot of punnets. Two for 60p!"

A couple of passing women stopped, eyes lighting on the offer.

"Cor, duck. We have some beau'iful tomatoes 'ere! Two pounds for 80p!"

Sipping tea, Mrs Wasson stood back, watching her son with amused pride as punters, attracted by the young man's performance, paused to purchase produce. This continued under an increasingly grey afternoon sky. A burst of summer rain sent people sheltering under canvas eaves of stalls, stooping between heavy drops of tumbling water. Rain hammered on the canvas over their heads as Joe and his mother were suddenly busy, selling off much of their fresh stock. The rain finally eased as the market day edged to a close, and people dispersed. A few remaining stragglers passed, eager for further reductions as stall holders began packing stock into vans. With his mum's encouragement, Joe made his final pitch. "Strawberry punnets, two for 60p!"

Pausing for a drink, Joe caught sight of a familiar figure at a nearby stall. Grabbing his mother's cap from the side, Joe pulled it low over his forehead. From the corner of his eye, Joe watched the college drama tutor, Mr Phillips. Joe busied himself arranging the last of the strawberry punnets.

The college tutor paused, ducking into their stall. Joe glanced up from his hands as Mr Phillips queried the price of tomatoes, gaining a muttered reply. Considering all choices, he settled his gaze to the strawberries.

Joe tugged his cap down. "Can I help you, guv?"

"Yes, strawberries, please. Those there." Leaning over to make his choice, Mr Phillips nudged a leg into a steel rod and instinctively stepped back. The stall shook, and a random rivulet of rain poured over his head and shoulders. Agitated, he leaned back but carried on with his choice of strawberries. "That one, please." Mr Phillips nodded.

Joe froze as the man's wet hairpiece flopped over his forehead, revealing a scalp of mottled skin that looked like a strange map. The dispirited fixing tape then gave way. The toupee fell and wedged between strawberry punnets. Mr Phillips's eyes bulged in disbelief. Joe dropped two punnets into a carrier, along with the retrieved, sodden hairpiece, and calmly handed him the bag.

"There you are, guv, have them on the 'ouse."

Mr Phillips didn't argue, grabbed the items, and sped, red-faced, away from the market.

Many stall holders, having seen the man's calamity, closed the day with amusement. Joe felt sorry for his college tutor. When he explained to his mum who Mr Phillips was, her amusement increased.

August gave way to September, and the first day of the course arrived. He began the day apprehensive about seeing Mr Phillips, thinking he might remember him from the market-day incident. Relief came as the drama tutor showed no apparent recollection on seeing him. It appeared that Mr Phillips had gained a far more secure new head of hair. Joe was empathetic as to why he might want to cover the large birthmark.

Other students were studying English, history, and social studies, as well as the business and construction trades, but Joe's core studies centred on theatre and drama. Apart from a couple of mature students in their late twenties, Joe found the remaining drama students close to his own age. He was one of six guys amid a majority of girls in their late teens.

Upon entering the classroom, everyone automatically divided into two sexes, the boys seated at neighbouring tables and the girls taking to the remaining seats at the front. With a loud clap of hands and a projected voice, Mr Phillips made everyone stand, and he rearranged the seating with the six boys scattered among the girls. Everyone seemed eager to talk, covering over any nerves with projected excitement.

Having first spoken to one of the boys, a tall, thin, curly-haired youth, Joe turned to the girl he was sat beside. Her eyes sparkled with restless excitement. Everyone's conversation was interrupted as they were told such a classroom situation would not be the norm, and much of their learning would take place in the performance hall.

First, everyone had to introduce themselves. They were to stand and address everyone with a summary of why they were on a drama course. Joe held his breath, trying to think why he was there. It seemed to be a repetition of the course audition, which he decided was how to approach the moment. Jennifer, Angela, David, Maria, and Adina took their turn. Joe stood and made his piece. One of them had already tried the joke of "I am an alcoholic," which fell flat, without the expected result of laughter. After which she got the nickname Alchy. Joe quickly decided not to make any such attempt. As he scanned the faces, Joe paused on one.

While not a mature student, he looked older than eighteen. He was stocky and wore a white T-shirt and stonewashed jeans. His dark hair was styled in keeping with the past decade: short back and sides, long on top, which he had habit of brushing back, though it stubbornly fell back over his brow. Joe fixed on his blue eyes and the slight smile that was returned. Joe's moment was suddenly over, and he quickly sat.

Stumbling over his words, Ben was cut short by Mr Phillips. Then three of the girls spoke. Linda, Susan, Julie. Then *he* stood up. Adam. How could it be anything else? His was a presence that looked suited to the garden of Eden. The young man had an olive complexion and watchful eyes, and he addressed them with a deep voice. His hair flopped again, but he made no attempt to brush it back as he told the group of his personal drama ambitions. After coming across as clear and confident, Adam calmly retook his seat with a smile. With some of the mystery of the handsome stranger resolved, Joe turned to concentrate on the others' introductions. Everyone spoke of similar ambitions, with the majority stating a desire to work in theatre, which likely satisfied Mr Phillips's background in treading the boards.

The first week passed in a whirl of newness. Much time was spent not in the classroom but in an old hall with a tatty-looking stage at one end, reminiscent of school nativity plays.

Joe joined the class, nervous about wearing his brother's old tracksuit, as they began with exercises to shed their inhibitions. Mr Phillips took no prisoners as he shouted instructions that they had to pretend to become an animal or creature of their choice. Joe became a clumsy rabbit, nibbling carrots and hopping about; being the third rabbit, all further rabbits were banned. Joe was aware of Adam from the start of the class and observed his persona of a grasshopper, his height making him look ungainly.

Similarly, Adam wore a too-large tracksuit, which was something they had in common. With each task, Joe purposely kept his distance from Adam, fearful of the young man's presence; being the best-looking student, confident, and popular with the tutor, his very being was intimidating. Then, close to the end of class, Joe had a renewal of excitement as he was paired with Adam. Other pairs were to act out farm animals or birds, but Adam and Joe were given the role of two apes. Following Adam's move, Joe sat on his haunches, appropriately grunted and scratched. Then Adam started to groom him. Slowly and then more keenly dipping fingers into his hair, gently plucking invisible creatures, nibbling on them, and looking for more in his imagined fur.

Joe felt a shiver run through him under his searching touch. Before their silent audience, Adam nudged him, roughly grunting how he wanted the favour returned. Joe softly cooed as he searched behind Adam's ear, combing back his long hair. It was the first time he had been so close to another man, softly touching his ear and neck. It was...intoxicating. Terrifying.

Engulfed by a bubble of excited confusion, Joe shivered at the pop of suppressed emotion as his feelings began to make sense. He had always had a fondness for girls, an admiration for their beauty—in the playground, at the age of five, he had proposed to a girl—but had never held any physical attraction for them. As he plucked invisible bugs off Adam, Joe began to feel the stir of instinct. The word gay, that at school that had been a demeaning insult, came to his thoughts.

A clap and the loud voice of the tutor made him jump. Joe toppled back onto his side.

Adam squeezed his shoulder. "Good one, mate, thanks."

As the first week concluded, he walked about in a heightened, thrilling sense of apprehension. Restless, Joe sought solace from his thoughts by helping his parents over the weekend. Yet unanswerable questions wrestled in his mind. An inner debate whirled. Why had he felt fixated by Adam? None of the other men on the course attracted him. Perhaps his feeling was unique to Adam.

During the unfolding days of an Indian summer, Joe found himself drawn into events.

The collective drama students began to project an unwelcome attitude around the college. Out of class, they formed cliques, hovering near the corners of the college premises. Arm in arm, the drama girls loitered, laughing and talking loudly, oblivious to fellow students. Equally, some of the boys strolled confidently about the building, brazen in their demand for attention. A few noisy drama students led to exclusions by an angry librarian. Despite them all facing their drama tutor's reprimand, a minority continued with their churlish behaviour.

Excited to be part of a fringe drama clan, Joe hung out with Ben, David, and best of all, Adam. They were the odd bods of the class. They sat together on the grass quadrant practising dialogues from Shakespeare and 1960s kitchen-sink dramas, as favoured by their course leader. Of all of them, Ben struggled to fit in. Bodily self-conscious, Ben was tall and thin with gangly limbs, his expression and eyes shadowed by a mop of unkempt, curly hair. Mr Phillips became openly frustrated with him, while some girls sniggered at Ben's attempts during classes. Yet Ben memorised his lines easily and was determined to work on his projection and expression. Adam and Joe encouraged Ben to build his confidence when working together in expression of monologues. Ben, though, remained clumsy around girls, struggling in classes when interacting with female students.

Frustration turned to anger as Joe witnessed the blatant lack of support for Ben by any of the drama tutors. Then, one day Ben was off sick, and he never came back.

Soon after, a further student dropped out for unknown reasons. By the end of the week, a new student joined their ranks, a Black girl called Cassie, who had transferred from a similar course in Birmingham. Attractive but somewhat shy, Cassie became an honorary member of the odd bods, taking Ben's place.

Joe shared a like-mindedness with girls which proved awkward at times. So far, he had muddled through classes involving romantic scenes. To others, it wasn't obvious, as he managed to be seen as straight. While he had started to become at ease with his crush on Adam, a conflict inhabited his head as he lacked any sexual attraction towards the female students.

Events soon took a turn for the worse.

Posters around the college advertised a fancy dress party for all students. They were to meet at the King's Head in town before going on to another venue. Two months into the college year, students were developing friendships and socialising. Joe was studying the poster over the shoulders of some social studies students when Adam appeared at his side.

"You going to the party, then?" asked Adam.

"Thinking about it. Sounds like a good idea to dress up."

"Could be. What would you go as?"

Joe felt Adam's hand rest on his shoulder, his breath bouncing off his ear. He trembled at the contact. "A gangster, maybe," said Joe, remembering all those old black and white movies he used to watch.

"Really? Like a 1930s mobster, a striped suit and trilby hat. Suppose that would be quite smart." He looked genuinely impressed.

"Will you be going?"

"When is it? Thursday...odd night for a party. Yeah, why not? Not sure what I could wear though. Consider it a date." Adam shook his shoulder a little for emphasis.

Joe was left stunned. *A date.* Wow.

The days leading up to the party dragged. A buzz went around the drama course about the fancy dress party. He caught snatches of conversations. A lot of people were going. Joe felt upbeat at the prospect of spending time with Adam, amid a mass of partygoers.

At last, the evening arrived. Joe had buzzed through the week with excited nerves. In the end, he decided to go for a cowboy look instead, nothing too extreme. His mum had helped with the costume by taking his dad's old denim jacket and sewing long fringes across the arms and back. Then, to go along with a worn pair of jeans, he'd bought a pair of cowboy boots. Best of all, his mum had a friend who owned a cowboy hat that had actually come from America. His mum folded paper into the inside band to make it fit, although most of the time he was going to hang it about his shoulders. A collarless shirt and a bandana around the neck completed the look.

While his mum was pleased that Joe looked like a cowboy, his dad was wary.

"Are you really going out looking like that?"

Joe was annoyed with his dad for their late arrival in town, even though he'd offered to drop him off. The slippery angled heels of his boots made for baby strides as Joe walked to the pub. He smiled to himself, thinking Adam would be there already, and envisioned him as a pirate. Anticipation jangled as he approached the pub, light spilling out the door where a number of punters stumbled out, juggling overfull pints.

Joe hesitated on wobbly heels as a tipsy woman pointed his presence out to others. The group openly laughed and jeered at the cowboy who entered the pub.

Pausing on the bar's threshold, Joe self-consciously looked into the over-lit room. Everywhere were groups of people standing or sitting at tables. He couldn't see any familiar faces or fellow students in fancy dress.

Someone pushed past him, looking him over, sharing a joke with his girlfriend. Maybe Joe could wait outside.

"After a drink, cowboy?"

Adam? Joe turned. But instead of a pirate, a young barman but older than himself, glanced at him then wiped the bar. After a moment, Joe relaxed and turned fully to the bar, tipping his hat onto his shoulders.

"Sarsaparilla or whisky?"

"What?" Joe frowned.

"Just a joke." The bartender rolled his eyes. "Wanna pint of–"

"Lager."

As the barman poured the drink, he studied Joe's outfit. "Are you sure you wanna be here? Not the best pub in town to dress like that."

"I'm meeting friends from college. We're meeting here then going on elsewhere. Have you seen anyone? They should be all dressed up."

The barman put the drink on the bar and took his money. "I did see maybe four girls. They were dressed up, but they didn't stay."

Joe took a nervous sip. Where were all the people who were supposed to be on this night out? "Did you see if there was a pirate?"

The barman grinned. "Sorry, no pirates."

Joe was left alone as the barman turned to serve others. Leaning back on the bar, he kept the glass to his lips as he again surveyed the pub, trying to pick out familiar people, dressed up or not. The pub lights were suddenly dimmed. A few random cheers echoed as some DJ in a corner started playing a chart hit.

Mixed with the sneaky swig of his dad's whisky he'd had for courage, Joe drank most of his pint. Relaxed by alcohol and the sudden sway of disco lights, he watched as pumping music led a number of people to a stained dance floor. With his cowboy presence no longer so obvious, Joe decided he would wait for Adam to appear. Surely, he'd show. *Someone* would come, wouldn't they? Another drink would help him relax. Joe turned to the bar but instead of the barman, a slim, fair-haired barmaid approached.

She winked. "Where's your horse, then?" Her red lips twisted with humour as she poured another lager.

"He's tethered outside," Joe said in a bad Texan accent. He emptied a third of the glass then moved away and stood close to an empty table, wondering where Adam was.

The dance floor had started to become crowded as another hit filled the air. Joe waited close to the door as more people entered. He stared, desperate to see a pirate. A number of young women in their late twenties broke into a shimmy as they entered, squealing with excitement as they headed straight to the dance floor.

Joe felt like the space was shifting about, his legs uncertain on unfamiliar heels. He pulled his hat back onto his head, cutting down the effect of the swirling red, yellow, and blue blasts of light. The women swirled on the edge of the dance floor. One of them fixed on him. She tottered towards Joe, took the half empty glass from his grasp, and slammed it onto the table.

"Hey, midnight cowboy! Come on and dance with us."

Reluctantly, Joe allowed the red-haired girl in a green dress to take his hand. He found himself spun among her friends, swaggering awkwardly in uncomfortable boots. Taking a deep breath, he let himself fall into the music, looking to bond and dance with the girls who seemed to just want a good time. The red-haired girl whooped as Joe copied her moves. Spinning wildly on his heels, Joe swayed to a halt. As he turned in time to the music, he saw a group of guys by the bar. Their watching, narrowed eyes were fixed on him. Joe spun with the beat, arms crossed. He turned again. As two of the guys leered at the girls, the third, shorter man glared at him. Joe looked away from the glare, but his stomach lurched with fear.

The red-haired girl in the green dress grabbed his hat, whooping as she threw it in the air. She passed it to her friend, who held it above her head. As the hat fell from her grasp, it was kicked between heeled shoes. Joe bent to grab the brim but missed it. Despite having drunk too much too fast, Joe made a sober protest trying to claim the hat back, but the girls ignored his appeal that the hat wasn't his. He chased the cowboy hat as it was grabbed by the girl in red, who held it on her styled bob cut, lapping up the admiration of her friends. In a quick manoeuvre, Joe got it back.

Flustered, he found the hot space suddenly crowded. At first, he didn't understand what was happening when the red-haired girl shoved away a guy who was too close to her, his hands gripping her waist. Still fixated on getting the redhead's full attention, she pushed the interloper back. Joe clenched the hat as one of the girls, trying to help her friend, tumbled into him. Stepping back, Joe stared frozen with anxiety as the shortest of the three guys turned on him.

Joe watched, anxiety mounting too slowly, as one of the guys from the bar turned on him.

"You fucking queer bastard! Staring at my arse."

Joe felt the force against his cheek throw him backwards, pain bursting through the background of inebriation. The floor rammed into his back. Joe held onto his face and pulled himself into a protective ball. Joe shuddered as someone grabbed his collar and pulled him up and away. He staggered to the toilets, pushing past jeering faces and taunts. He stared at the damage in the mirror. His head pounded as outside the clamour finally abated. He had to leave. He had to get out. Emerging a few minutes later, Joe bumped into the barman, who winced on seeing him.

"You okay, mate?" The barman handed the Stetson to Joe. "That guy's just been carted off by the coppers. He's a troublemaker, ain't your fault. You should get off home though."

Swaying, Joe explained that his dad had given him a lift. There was supposed to be a party, friends to be with, but no one had shown up. After a moment's thought, the barman spoke to his manager, who said he could take Joe home. Half an hour later, Joe found himself dropped off at the gate. There'd been no conversation, explanations, judgement, or questions.

The barman gave a final smile, advising that he should get a bag of ice on the swelling and avoid the King's Head in future. "Afraid the King's Head isn't for the likes of you, cowboy." He turned his car and drove away into darkness.

Joe crept upstairs unheard, stripped the costume off, and threw it in a heap in the corner. He slept fitfully, the memory of that fist coming at him, the shoes all around his prone form, making him sweat and bringing tears to his eyes.

The reactions at breakfast were unavoidable and predictable. His mum's face fell at his bruised cheek and cut lip. While his mum fired questions at him, his dad's raised eyebrow was accompanied by a calm sip of tea and a wry smile.

"Could have told you not to go to that pub. It's always had a reputation for trouble," said his dad.

"Joe, did you get in a fight or..." His mum didn't seem to know the words to ask the obvious question.

"I was pushed and hit a table, that's all." Joe slumped at the breakfast table, repeating the near truth until his mum eventually ceased.

His mum sighed. "Hindsight's a wonderful thing."

His dad rolled his eyes. They knew of his mum's fondness in quoting sayings. There was silence as they ate, and Joe's face ached as he chewed.

After his dad left the kitchen, Joe's mum focused her narrowed eyes on him.

"Hindsight, Joe. What I mean is," said his mum. "That if we... if you don't try things, you won't know what's around the corner, will you? Even if it doesn't work out. Like your drama course. I'm proud you've taken a brave step to do what you want."

She took a bag of frozen peas from the freezer and pressed it gently to the swelling. She agreed that if he didn't feel like going to college, he could stay off till Monday.

Only later, when he was alone with his dad working in one of the polytunnels, did Joe confess to being punched.

As he set to watering the crop of lettuce, his dad slowly nodded. "Well, lad, you're old enough to fight, and if you go around dressing like a ponce, then you can only expect to attract trouble."

Joe frowned, unsure what to make of his dad's blunt reaction. Not exactly supportive but not an outright dismissal either. They let the subject drop and concentrated on lettuce.

Over the weekend, he retreated to his room, playing discs and listening to the radio, trying to distract his mind, but the question was on a loop. Had he really been so obvious? The thug's words kept ringing out. "You fucking queer bastard." And the barman's warning, "Not for the likes of you.." Even his dad had said that Joe had looked "like a ponce." Joe studied himself in the mirror, checking if his wrists were limp. They weren't. Nor did he have a camp walk. The bruise countered any such appearance; he looked more like a boxer.

As the pain eased, Joe brooded on the fact that Adam nor the other students had appeared. Was the whole thing a prank to see what idiot would go into one of the town's worst pubs? But Adam? He had promised to meet him. He hardly knew anything about him, nor did he have a phone number. Maybe Adam had played him for a fool.

With his return to college on Tuesday, the bruise had become a bluish splotch. Helping to overcome his anxiety, Joe's mum skimmed the site with cosmetics so that only the cut lip was most visible. Disapprovingly, his dad shook his head and said he should just wear the wound.

Joe walked into class, aware of speculative mutterings passing between students as they saw through the uneven makeup. The morning was spent studying the history of drama and acting theory. He kept his head down and avoided eye contact.

Adam arrived late and glanced back at Joe, who made no response to his double take. Joe made a sharp exit as the class ended, aware of Adam following him. Having decided to wash off his mum's makeup, he paused outside and leaned into the corner of the building, wanting but dreading seeing Adam appear. But he didn't. As usual, the afternoon was given over to students' leisure activities, followed by free period. Joe grabbed a sandwich and walked slowly to the swimming baths. As Adam preferred the running club, Joe felt safe from any encounter. Anger made him want to confront Adam, but shame made him want to hide. No one talked about the fancy dress party, and he couldn't bring himself to ask what had happened. Better not to admit he'd been a fool.

Reaching the edge of the pool, Joe panted with the exertion from half a dozen lengths. He faced the edge of the pool, blotting out the presence of other swimmers. Treading water, he meditated on the reflections of overhead lights distorted by the wavering blue surface. Buffeted by the force of swimmers pushing themselves into another length, Joe rested. Ducking into the water to prepare for another bout of lengths, Joe emerged facing the head and shoulders of a swimmer.

Removing black goggles, Adam smiled at him. "Hi."

Combined surprise and tension resulted in Joe grimacing as pain and made him gasp.

"What's up?" Adam frowned, treading water.

"Cramp...my leg." He slipped beneath the surface.

Hands grasped his waist and lifted him from the water onto the side. With his leg involuntary locked, Joe glanced at Adam exiting the pool, revealing his lean body. The darting pain distracted him as he found himself being manoeuvred from the edge. The same firm hands that had lifted him from the water began massaging his calf. Joe breathed as the muscle relaxed. No one in the pool seemed to take notice as the first aider continued longer than needed.

"Better?" Adam's gaze was intense and searching as he met Joe's eyes.

"Yeah, thanks."

Adam nodded and slipped back into the water, leaving Joe to process what had just happened, his relaxed leg retaining the memory of Adam's touch.

Holding onto the rail, Adam looked up at Joe, whose gaze wandered over him.

"What are you doing here?" Joe steadied his breathing. "Thought you preferred running to swimming."

"Yeah, well, I wanted to apologise, but you seemed to be avoiding me earlier. Cost me a pair of trunks and goggles to get this far."

They both looked under water. "Very tropical looking trunks. Not that you'd catch me in them."

Adam's eyes glinted as if he was about to say something but decided otherwise.

"They were all they had. Last week, I'm sorry, it was Mum. She fell down the stairs, and I had to get her to the hospital. Dad was working and I had to get us a taxi and–"

"Right." The excuse sounded feeble, no matter how much he wanted to believe it.

"It happened as I was about to leave, and there was no way to let you know. You must have seen the others. Did you have a good time?"

"No." Joe brooded, unconsciously pressing his bruised cheek. It was hard to remain angry at someone who floated before him, looking genuinely concerned.

"So, what happened?"

"Nothing." He didn't want to say it.

"Something to do with that bruiser, I'm guessing." Adam pointed at his cheek. "C'mon. What happened?"

Joe fixed on Adam's stare. "Some bigoted idiot hit me."

"Bigoted?" Adam floated closer.

Joe took a slow breath. The activity in the pool had moved to the shallow end. He made a rapid study of Adam's eyes and took a gamble. "Called me a 'fucking queer' just before thumping me."

"Right," said Adam, dipping his chin in the water, though his gaze never wavered.

"Thing is, he was right. I am gay." Joe felt a surge of electricity sweep through him on his impulsive confession. He had never told anyone. To say gay aloud was shocking. What had he done? It would change everything between them.

A movement from the pool interrupted the moment. A dark shape lifted from the water, and Cassie gave them a brilliant smile, her ebony skin and dark plaited hair glistening from the water and over-bright light.

"What are you boys up to?" She clasped the rail close to Joe and flipped back her hair with elegant fingers.

"Nothing, nothing. Joe here managed to get cramp," Adam said quickly.

"Thought so. I saw you nursing him." She smiled with a tilted expression, studying their awkward tension. "How about a race? I need the motivation." Cassie looked down the pool where two roped sections had become free as a few swimmers vacated the pool. "You too, if your leg has recovered."

"Go on then," said Adam, as if it were a question to Joe.

Joe perched on the pool's perimeter and shook his head. "I'll play judge and time you."

Moving into place, Cassie asked Adam if he could do the back stroke. Adam said he could do anything she challenged him to.

"On your marks!" Joe raised his hand and tried to keep it from shaking. He watched as they returned and pushed into another length, Cassie just ahead. Leaving them mid-race, Joe hurried his shower. Showering quickly, he knew he had to get out of there before Adam followed, certain of his rejection for admitting that he was gay. Cold air hit him as he left the sports centre and started his brooding, lonely walk to the bus.

Hindsight Is a Wonderful Thing

"Hold up!"

Joe kept walking across the car park. He glanced back and saw Adam emerge from the glass and concrete centre. A chemical cloud of steam followed him. Joe increased his pace, but Adam easily caught him up.

"Hey, what's the rush?"

"No rush." Joe slowed his pace, trying to appear as though nothing was bothering him. "Where's Cassie?"

"Cassie's having a coffee. Think she's waiting for a friend. Did you want one? A coffee?" Adam adjusted his rucksack and kicked at a stone.

"No." Joe set off again, not knowing what else to say.

"Okay." Adam walked closer, so their sleeves brushed.

Joe nervously edged away from the contact. "What I said back there. Adam, I'm not sure...my head's confused, probably from that punch." Like a paper cut to his soul, the lie hurt.

"I'm sorry about what happened to you. Pretty shit. Fancy a walk so you can talk about it?"

"I'm going home."

"We don't have to go far. I feel really bad about not showing up at the party. Turns out, the others met up on the street, and they went somewhere else and picked up others along the way. It was damn bad luck you missed them."

Joe stopped and looked at him. Perhaps it would help. Deciding Adam looked sincere, he agreed.

Adam led him a short distance, turning into a cul-de-sac after passing some neglected-looking council houses. On reaching a finger sign hanging by a single nail on an aged sun-bleached post, they climbed over a broken fence. They walked a narrow footpath that emerged from undergrowth into open fields that marked the town's edge. He relaxed as they left the streets behind them. Open spaces had a calming effect on him.

As they walked, Joe described what happened that night and how the barman took him home.

"Sounds like a decent guy, this barman. I know that pub can be a bit dodgy, though usually at weekends."

"That's what my dad said. I'd never heard of it before." Relief flowed over him as he shared how scared he'd been, how he felt lucky the barman had been supportive and a decent guy instead of a bigot like the others. Adam nodded thoughtfully and let him talk.

A sheen of autumn had descended across the countryside. The uneven, overgrown path snaked the edge of a bank of trees, hiding the main line to London. Joe assumed the path was rarely used. A grey shape of a train rumbled northwards.

"How far are we going?"

"Nearly there." Adam pushed a branch out of the way.

A hundred yards ahead, Joe saw an old, red brick bridge taking the rail line over a stream. Joe caught up to Adam on the bank. There was no obvious way they could cross the width of water that followed the edge of the fields beyond.

"How do we get across?"

"We don't. Come on," said Adam.

The dry, earthy path led them under the gloomy brick archway. Joe studied the curved, graffiti-covered walls. He wondered how the creators had managed to cross to the other bank and reach several feet above their heads. The town's houses lay at a distance beyond fenced fields. Dropping his bag at his feet, Adam leaned against the Victorian infrastructure.

"This is where you live?" asked Joe, watching Adam produce a battered packet of cigarettes. His face flared gold by a struck match. "You smoke?"

"Sometimes. Want one?"

"No, thanks. Bad for you, aren't they?"

"Probably. But when you're an actor, you've got to be prepared to do anything. If you want to get a part, and it means smoking, gotta get used to it."

"Right." Choosing a sliver of the wall devoid of spray paint, Joe leaned against it. He shook his head again at the proffered cigarettes.

"I used to come here to think. There's never anyone around."

"Except for the odd graffiti artist, by the looks of it." A nervous excitement took hold as a surge of anxiety replaced the calm of walking through open spaces with his companion. Adam was good-looking. Nearly all the female students talked about him. Why had he let Adam bring him here? Maybe he planned to beat him up, finish what that thug in the pub started. He thought they were becoming friends, but that could change. Joe swallowed as he thought he might need to run. Slowly, he took a few steps away, pausing at the bridge's perimeter.

"I think you should know," said Adam, but the sentence hung in the air, and he bit his lip, clearly thinking about something.

"Know what?" Joe asked sharply.

"Adam isn't my real name. My full name is Jorge Matias Adan Moreno. I decided on Adam as my stage name."

Joe raised his eyebrow. So, there wasn't going to be any kind of scuffle. Just a disclosure of personal history. Strange, but okay. "Doesn't sound very English."

"It's not."

"Italian?"

"No, Spanish," said Adam and smiled.

"You don't have an accent." Aware of an almost accusatory tone, Joe lowered his shoulders. "You sound like a proper Midlands guy to me."

"I was born in Spain, but my parents moved to the UK when I was a baby. My brother was five. He still has a trace of an accent. I was worried what you might think."

"Wow." Looking at him in a new light, the lack of English features or pale skin made sense. Now, he looked exotic.

"Wow," Adam imitated him. "You're impressed then? Can't say I've had such an amazing reaction before."

"I've never met anyone from abroad." Joe kicked a shower of stones into the shallow ditch. "Why come to the UK from Spain? Think I'd rather be in Spain."

"I was a baby, so no choice, I'm afraid. My parents lived around Montefrio. They were Romas."

"Romas?"

"You probably know such people as gypsies."

Joe turned from the view to study Adam again, taking in the dark brown hair and broody eyes.

"You live in a caravan then?"

"No." Adam's smile faded, and he shook his head. "My parents left Spain twenty years ago. I think they were a bit rebellious at the time, and they ran off together and got married even though their parents were against it. They settled in the Midlands, and my dad started a business. He owns a couple of restaurants."

Joe mentally went through town. There was a restaurant on the main street. "Mesa de Comida."

"That's right. Dad has another in Nottingham."

Adam flicked the cigarette stub into the green water, where it fizzed and died.

Joe glanced at him. "So, Jorge, why did you–"

A sudden thundering of an intercity train pelted over their heads, taking commuters to Nottingham or maybe Leicester. They waited until the rush passed.

"I prefer to be called Adam." He looked sideways at Joe.

Joe stared ahead, studying the brickwork. "Why tell me now?"

"We've known each other for a few weeks and... I wanted to..." Adam faltered. "We all have our secrets, Joe."

Joe looked at Adam's hand that had clasped his forearm. He tugged at him so they moved into the shadow of the bridge. The evening was starting to fall.

"You told me your secret, and I wanted you to know I'm...I'm also..."

Joe instinctively knew what was about to happen as Adam pressed him against the graffiti-covered bricks. Adam's cautious lips touched his, hesitating as Joe flinched with the pain of his cut lip. He found himself breathing quicker as Adam's fingers rested on his bruised cheek. He inhaled cigarette breath and the leather of his creaking biker jacket. He breathed in freedom and found himself in Adam's embrace.

They were deaf to the *thunk, thunk* of the clanking above. The only sound Joe registered was the beating of his heart as it thudded in time with Adam's.

To Eat a Starving Dog

Rebecca Summerscales

You don't bother to kill it.
Its eyes follow you, legs still,
the nub of its tail attempting a pathetic little wag.
You hear in its sigh the moment
it realises - realises you are alike
with its twitching nose, like Morse code
it tells you there is a version of events where you are the dog
and what would you ask of it, then?
It tells you of every ball it has ever chased,
every pat on its little head, every bone it ever gnawed on.
It knows you are alike. You bite down. Hear a whimper.
You see an intimacy in the fear,
how all dying eyes are all-seeing. There is
something in the whites that keeps this
between you both. You will be hungry again, later.

The Dinner Party

Laura Martin

HERE I AM AT the world's most boring dinner party. Well, I shouldn't be so unkind, it's me who's the boring one. I don't have anything new to report I'm afraid, just boring old me, still single, working (just about), and still living with my parents.

"Yes, just waiting on my house to complete."

"No, I'm not dating anyone right now."

"That's wonderful that your son/daughter/husband/*dog* is having a baby/getting married/has a new job, I'm abso-fucking-lutely thrilled for them."

The responses escape my mouth but I'm somewhere else, dreaming of the life I long for. I'm not usually like this, I promise you. I'm a social butterfly. I'll talk to anyone and everyone. Sharing a joke with a shop cashier, hearing an old man's life story on the bus, grinning at a woman who tripped and happened to catch my eye... a secret shared between strangers.

But not here. Not tonight. At least the food is good. My mum's homemade beef bourguignon, tender slow-cooked chunks of gorgeousness and the crispiest roasties, golden brown with insides as fluffy as a cloud! And dessert is profiteroles, light, and airy, and drenched in heavenly, rich dark chocolate sauce. I have a second helping since my ex is no longer here to ask, "Laura, do you really need that?" I mean, who doesn't need a second profiterole when they're this good?

"Laura. Laura?"

It takes me a few moments to realise that I'm daydreaming, and the room comes back into focus.

"Laura, if you could invite anyone alive or dead to a dinner party, who would you invite?"

I'm always unsure how to answer these things. Would Jesus be offended if I left him off the guest list? What about my grandad, who I only knew for the first seven years of my life? I try to think of a witty and clever response but eventually I say, "Anne Lister." A few puzzled faces stare back at me. God, how I wish I was anywhere else. "*Gentleman Jack*?" I say almost hopefully.

"Oh, the BBC series?"

He must have seen it advertised whilst searching for something to watch. I feel quite certain he wouldn't spend his oh-so-precious time on something about women.

"Yes, that's right. She was a fascinating character and wrote her diaries in a cryptic code that has only just been uncovered."

"Interesting choice," he replies and wanders off.

He evidently doesn't find this remotely interesting, because he rushes to tell everyone his answer to the question he has just posed. Clearly, his answer is far more clever and interesting than mine. I want another profiterole. I sneak another one onto my plate before anyone notices.

Aargh, I think with a sigh, Anne Lister. How amazing it would be to meet her. I'd fallen in love with her in the very first episode of *Gentleman Jack* and even deeper in love since reading her translated diaries. How ridiculous, right? How can you fall in love with a historical figure? Oh, how I wish I could have met her. I find a quiet, empty corner and fall deeper and deeper into this wonderful daydream...

Bewildered, I blink against the light. What's going on? I was at my parents' dinner party and suddenly I'm here all alone. Surely, I didn't drink *that* much, did I? I feel spaced out and strange, as if awoken from a dream but I'm not sure if I'm still dreaming or not. I'd been dreaming about Anne Lister.

The clock strikes seven and the loud *ding dong* of the doorbell startles me. What the heck? It was almost ten in the evening just now. I'd been counting down the minutes until I could get ready for bed, I was that bored. I check my phone, which also says 19:00. I'm baffled. I've heard of losing time but never of it going backwards. But everything else is off, too. No boring dinner party guests showing how clever they are. No mound of profiteroles. Just me and a sense of anticipation I don't understand. The doorbell rings again. My insides feel like jelly, and my heart is racing. I'd been imagining all the details in my head just now, thinking of what we would eat, what we would talk about, and what time she would arrive. Seven. Everything has a surreal quality that leaves me breathless. I'm hesitant to open the door. Is she really out there? Will she think this rather odd? What if she finds me boring and dull? *Oh, for goodness sake, Laura, just open the damn door.*

As I approach the door, my heart is in my mouth. And then, there she is. I stand with my mouth agape, in awe of her presence. Her face is a little rounder than I'd imagined, but the darkest and most caring eyes stare back at me. I'm pleased to see she's dressed entirely in black, apart from a champagne silk India handkerchief around her neck. She looks exquisite. She holds her head up high, with perfect posture, her back straight, exuding confidence and pride. Her confidence and charm make me feel quite emotional. I'm reminded of my ex, Qasida, who also tended to dress in a more masculine style but couldn't fully embrace who she was, held hostage to the strong gender norms of her Indian heritage.

Anne smiles. "Excuse me, I have been invited to a dinner party at a Miss Martin's house this evening at seven o'clock. Please can you advise me if this is the correct residence?"

"Yes, yes, that's me. Although please call me Laura." I don't care how bizarre this is. I'm going to run with it and see where it leads. I step aside so she can enter. The house is my parents', but since there's no one else here, I pretend it's my own.

"What a pretty name. It's a pleasure to make your acquaintance."

"May I ask, Miss Lister, how you got here? And...umm...how did you know my address?" The question feels silly as it comes off my lips. We're not even in the same century. But here she is, so I have to know.

"Well, it was rather a long journey down from Halifax, I'm afraid. It did take a couple of days in all, but the company in my carriage, a newly-wed young couple travelling down to London for their honeymoon, I found to be quite pleasant, and they took quite an interest in learning about my travels abroad. Your address is quite clearly shown here on the invitation delivered to me last week. Oh, and please, do call me Anne."

"I'm not sure how it could have been delivered to you last week, I only thought of inviting you just this evening, and I never imagined you would actually come."

She waves the invitation a tad impatiently. "I couldn't turn down an invitation to meet 'a woman from the future,' could I? The invitation intrigued me greatly. I couldn't quite believe such a thing could be possible, but here I am."

Sure. Why not? She time-travelled in a carriage, just to meet me.

Implausible or not, I liked it. "And what did you imagine this 'woman of the future' would be like?" *Please say me*.

"I was unsure. I had hoped you wouldn't be one of those people parading about the town in their undergarments, as I witnessed on my way down here into the future. It was quite a sight to behold, men wearing nothing but trousers with no shirt or coat, and women wearing only their drawers and a short chemise. I am glad to see you have dressed suitably for the occasion."

I look down and smile to myself. It has been one of the hottest days of the year today. There would have been plenty of bare flesh on show. Thank goodness I had worn one of my longer and more modest dresses.

"So, tell me, Laura, what possessed you to invite me to your dinner party, of all people?" She sits on my sofa and looks around, as though taking in all the differences of our times.

"Well, I first heard about you through a television series. You're played by an incredible actress, and I later read your translated diaries."

Her eyes widen. "My diaries were translated? Not all of it, surely? Some of it was written in my cryptic hand."

She doesn't ask what a TV is, and I'm glad, as I don't want to have to explain it. "All of it was translated, even your cryptic hand, which they've been able to decipher. It's incredibly fascinating."

Anne sits very still, looking perplexed and quite shocked. I hadn't exactly planned out this conversation in my head, and I was beginning to worry Anne wouldn't take this news very well.

After what feels like an age, Anne says, "So when were these translated? I sincerely hope my family and the people of Halifax were not witness to this. There was surely enough gossip and talk in the town as it was."

"No, no, the diaries were only translated very recently, and the world is very different now. Some of the things you speak about in your diaries, well, they wouldn't cause the gossip and negativity the way it did back then." I attempted to reassure her, but I couldn't imagine what it would feel like to know the world had read your most private thoughts.

"So," she says slowly and carefully, "a woman is allowed to express her love for another of the fairer sex?"

"Yes, absolutely, and not just that. It's even written in law that a person is allowed to love another freely, regardless of their gender. And we're allowed to marry now. Isn't that incredible?"

Once again, she looks bemused. "Goodness, I had dreamed of being able to do just that. How extraordinary. So, the Protestant church allow two women or men to marry?"

"Well, not yet. There's still some way to go when it comes to the church, but we're allowed to have a civil ceremony, a marriage as legally binding as a church wedding."

"Hmm. Are you married, Laura?" She studies me, almost like she's studying a new species.

"I'm afraid not. I was due to be married but unfortunately the engagement was broken just last year."

"Oh, I am terribly sorry. I don't wish to intrude, but how did it break?"

I pause, unsure if Anne really wants to hear my story. I was more fascinated to learn more about her. But why not? I had nothing to lose. "I'll get us a glass of wine and tell you all about it."

Anne sits in the lounge, waiting for me to bring through a glass of wine for us both. She looks around in awe at the furniture and décor, perhaps admiring the modern changes to style that had occurred over the last two hundred odd years. Carefully, she sits down on the sofa so as not to disturb the perfectly plumped pillows.

"Here we are, a glass of the finest Argentinian Malbec."

"Thank you, Laura. How lovely. I've never had wine from Argentina before." Anne smiles and raises her eyebrows to show her appreciation. "So, tell me all about this engagement, then." Anne tips her head slightly to the side, and her beautiful dark eyes look directly into mine.

I'm entranced, as if the rest of the world doesn't exist. It's only us in this moment. "Um, well, it's a long story. Are you sure you've got time to hear it?" What does time even mean at this point?

"Well, we've got all evening. And since you already know about me, I want to find out about you."

Do I want to tell my life story to the woman I've been secretly idolising? I guess it's only fair. After all, I do know all about her. "Okay. We actually met on the internet," I say, suddenly aware that Anne won't know what the internet is. "It's sort of like an electronic newspaper, where adverts are put out to help you find a romantic interest."

"Ahh, how extraordinary. Wonderful."

"Yes, it is, although some individuals are looking for other types of interest, if you know what I mean." I feel my face grow hot. Why had I felt the need to mention that?

"Oh goodness, surely not? That sounds like prostitution. These people do *not* pay for that, do they?"

"Some do, but not me." Given her horrified expression, I hurry to reassure her. "Although it was quite a challenge to sort out those who are looking for love and those...other ones. It's not always immediately obvious from their advert."

"Oh dear, that sounds quite a challenge."

"Yes, it was, but nevertheless I persevered until I found Qasida. We shared some written messages back and forth for a couple of months. We would have arranged to meet in person earlier, but she planned to go back to her home country of India over the Christmas holiday. We met in person in January of 2017."

"This new way of courting sounds quite astonishing. I'm not sure if it makes finding love easier or more difficult. It sounds like there is much to consider." She swirls the wine in her glass, staring into it contemplatively, trying to make sense of what she'd been told.

"Absolutely, it is difficult, but the positive thing is that all people can state exactly what they're looking for. Male, female, whatever, certain ages, location within the country, and so forth. Qasida stayed about three quarters of an hour away from me. She was living with her father in London whilst studying for her master's degree, although her heart was always in India." Saying it out loud makes my heart ache a little.

"So, you did not live together?"

Anne seems to search my expression. I wonder what she sees. "Not at first. For the first year or so, she lived in London. I would visit her, or she would visit me, and the initial months were so much fun and so exciting. I had never been involved with anyone before, female or male. I knew I had feelings for the same sex for years, but I never felt comfortable enough to fully explore it. I'm sure you can relate to growing up in a community where heterosexual relationships are the norm; it takes some time to feel fully at ease with your own identity."

"Oh, yes." Anne smiles wistfully. "Although my wish to be with a woman was granted, I was never able to fully be at ease with my identity. We had to tell others we were 'companions,' which we were in some sense, but it was a façade. We could never share any intimate details with others. I find it incredible that you can do so now. Tell me more about Qasida."

"Ah, she was–or is, should I say, beautiful. I remember meeting her for the first time, and she was on the telephone to a friend when I greeted her. Normally, I would have considered that incredibly rude, but not with her. I was awestruck. She was even more attractive than I'd seen in her photographs. She has beautiful, coffee cream coloured skin, and she's often mistaken for being Spanish or European due to the lightness of her skin tone. She has the most beautiful big, brown eyes and a mischievous smile that makes me blush. We ordered a drink and some chips, and I tentatively asked, 'Shall I put vinegar on just my side or all over?' She said, 'All over' and told me she loved vinegar. I realised then that she was the one for me. A fellow vinegar lover!"

"She sounds lovely." Anne glances at the clock and then back to me.

I nod, ignoring the lump in my throat. "She made me feel so at ease, so comfortable. I'd never felt so comfortable with someone I was attracted to before. She was so charming and flirty. She raised an eyebrow when she asked me if I'd ever been with a woman before. I told her I hadn't, but that I wanted to." I stop for a moment and take a sip of wine as the memories flood through me. "I was hesitant though. I hadn't been with anyone before, and I didn't want to get my heart broken. My friends and family told me to take things slowly, not to rush into anything, but I couldn't argue with my heart. She had taken it."

"So how long were you together?" Anne asks.

"Almost five years, and they were the best and worst years of my life. I was so proud to call her my girlfriend and later, my fiancée. She was so outgoing, charming, and always respectful of anyone older than her, which I admired. I remember when my parents first met her, my mum had just had an operation on her ankle, and she rushed to help her open the door whilst she was navigating the lounge standing on just one leg! My family absolutely adored her from that first moment. I don't know how but she worked her way into everyone's hearts, and she could do nothing wrong. She was the first person my gran allowed to take a drink into her jacuzzi, and believe me, my gran is very particular about her jacuzzi. She also smoked cigarettes, and although she would smoke them away from the house and company, my family were surprisingly accepting of it. Even more than I was."

"So, when did your relationship start to change?"

"That's difficult to say. There was always a little more pressure when her family were involved, and they certainly became more so towards the end of our relationship. Also, there was a global pandemic, and it was significantly worse a couple of years ago. Qasida and her family couldn't travel to see one another, or they were stuck living here without being able to go back to India. Worst of all, there were many months where Qasida was in India, not being able to return to me."

"Good heavens, that sounds incredibly hard." Anne looks at me with her dark, understanding eyes. "Please tell me more. Things changed after this pandemic?"

"We had our ups and downs even before that. Initially, we couldn't tell her family about our relationship, which was difficult. I hated keeping our love a secret, and I wasn't used to hiding so much. I don't like being dishonest. Well, I'm not sure anybody does, but it made me feel anxious and upset that we couldn't be ourselves with them. Even at the end of our relationship, there were some distant family members who still didn't know about us, even though we were due to be married."

"You sound quite surprised and upset about that. Did you not have to hide to your family and friends?" She looks dubious, which makes sense.

"Not at all. I'm incredibly lucky to have very supportive family and friends. It's not been easy coming to terms with my own identity, but those who know who I am have never shown anything but love towards me."

"It sounds like there are many more people like yourself these days where these relationships are accepted by those around them."

"Absolutely, and in terms of gender identity too. A person's gender is viewed as being on a spectrum now, with some people feeling as if their gender is fixed and for others, it's more fluid and some days they identify more with being one or the other gender."

"How astonishing. What a revolutionary thought." Anne looks down and stays silent for a few moments. "I think I must be one of those people who has some fluidity to their gender. I was born a woman, but I certainly don't feel like one a lot of the time."

It must have been so hard to be her in a time when roles were so rigid. "I think you would be surprised at how many people feel the same way. Times have significantly changed, and people are starting to understand more about gender and some of the issues that arise around it. Although there's still some way to go; there needs to be more education and representation. I see more advertisements now with same-sex relationships, and I think the same needs to happen for those with different gender identities too. Things have evolved over time and hopefully, they will continue to do so."

"This evening is turning into a rather fascinating one. How enlightening and heartening to know how things are developing for the better."

"Absolutely!"

Anne checks her pocket watch. "Do excuse me, Laura, but I thought I had been invited to a dinner party. Can I ask when dinner will be?"

I look down at my phone. Shit, it's half past eight. I didn't realise we'd been talking for so long, and how rude of me. I hadn't even thought about food. I have no idea what we have in. My mum had the dinner ready for eight but that was before. How could I not have thought about that? You can't invite someone to a dinner party without actually cooking dinner. But then, I didn't actually invite her, did I? The room spins a little then rights itself again. I need to sort some food out.

"I'm sorry, Anne, excuse me. I wasn't sure if you would come tonight, so I'm not sure about dinner. I'll check what we have." I fumble for words, for excuses, for a way to explain that I didn't invite her and didn't have time to prepare anything before she came. "Sorry, this must seem very odd. I'll be back in a moment."

As I'm walking back to the kitchen to check what we have in for me to cook for dinner, I hear a loud ding. What the heck was that? It sounds like the oven timer, but we never use that thing. Entering the kitchen, I see the slow cooker is on. What the? I can see and smell my mum's beef bourguignon in there bubbling away. What kind of magic is this? How is this all even possible? I'm here speaking to Anne Lister, who lived over two hundred years ago, and whom I apparently invited to a dinner party. And the dinner is already prepared. How? And that sound *was* the oven. My mum's roast potatoes, looking as perfectly golden as ever. I breathe a sigh of relief. When I see my mum again, I'll kiss her a hundred times. She's saved me! Although, obviously I can't say thanks for preparing a meal for someone who lived two centuries ago. I'll deal with that later.

I return to the lounge. "If you'd like to take a seat at the dining table, I'll shortly be serving dinner."

"Ah, delightful." Anne walks over and takes a seat at the table already set out for two. Again, strange.

I plate up the food and bring it out to the table. It all looks perfect, just as it did when my mum brought it out previously, and strangely enough, I'm hungry again. I mean, I'm always hungry, but I wouldn't usually be so porky and go for two dinners in one night.

"This looks delicious; did you make it?" Anne asks.

"No, my mother did. I can cook but she's amazing, especially at roast potatoes."

"So, we were talking about gender before. Did Qasida feel more like a man or a woman?"

"She felt like a woman, although I'm not sure she had permission to be or feel any different. Her mother often tried to put makeup on her or get her to wear more feminine clothing, but she was never comfortable doing that. She had to wear very feminine dresses to Indian functions, and her mother would choose them all and get them fitted to her measurements."

"Goodness, it sounds like her mother was rather controlling." She made a noise of appreciation as she took her first bite of a roast potato.

"You could say that. Qasida was always so uncomfortable in those long, heavy, sparkly, pretty dresses, and I could never understand why she endured wearing them when she disliked them so much. She just said that she had to, and that was that. She said it was because of the Indian culture, that she had to be seen this way at formal occasions, and she never wanted to offend or upset her mother. Her mother always seemed to be too proud, too worried about the opinions of others and very concerned with her own self-image." I shrug. "I thought so, anyway."

"That must have been hard to deal with. It sounds like you really wanted her to be able to express herself in the way she wanted."

"Absolutely, just like you do. Well, I assume so. In the television series, you're portrayed as dressing and acting very much as you wish." Again, she looks a little puzzled, and I mentally slap myself for using terminology she won't understand. But how do you explain our world without talking technology?

"I can dress how I wish a great deal of the time, but not in my early life. As a child, my mother and father always put in me in the brightest, frilliest gowns they could possibly find. Of course, as I gained some independence, and now have the support of my uncle and aunt, I can dress as I wish. People quite often remark on how much I'm like a man. Although I must wear some ridiculous gowns at formal occasions, even in the presence of close friends. It's expected that I must 'dress up.'"

I picture what I've seen of her in the show. "Did you feel uncomfortable in those gowns?"

"Oh, yes, terribly so. I try to pick dark colours, black, blues, or perhaps purple, which I'm somewhat more comfortable in, but on those occasions, I can't wait to get back to wearing my usual attire. Qasida was very similar to me in that respect?"

"Yes, although of course, the fashions have changed over time. But she certainly felt more comfortable in a shirt and trousers, or in a traditional Indian kurta and salwar, a long top and loose-fitting trousers, tapered at the ankle."

"That sounds very comfortable, and cool to wear in the hot Indian climate."

I can't help picturing her, and it makes my heart ache. "Absolutely. She was very proud to wear Indian clothing, which I loved. She never wore a sari though, which is a very feminine Indian dress, and I never heard her mother trying to get her to wear one either, which was surprising." I'd never thought to ask her why that was. Now I wouldn't know.

"Ah, and you like to dress in a more feminine way?" She looks me over.

"I love beautiful clothing and jewellery. I'm a magpie; I love anything sparkly!" I hope it doesn't make me sound shallow. Her smile makes me feel better about my admission.

"You look wonderful tonight. So, when did things end with Qasida?"

"November last year. She'd only returned to England just over two weeks prior to that. She acted very strangely, not showing any love or affection, and getting dressed and undressed with her body hidden. It was odd, and it sent my anxiety through the roof."

"What made you feel so anxious?"

The rush of old anxiety, feeling like a grip tightening around my heart, filled me. "I was still very deeply in love with her, although there were so many signs that something was wrong, now that I look back, and I realise that she didn't have the courage to tell me her true feelings. Even on the day we split, I had to force her into telling me what she wanted to do. It felt like a plaster over a wound which she was pulling off bit by bit, catching every hair. I told her if there wasn't a future for us, she needed to rip off that plaster and free me from the wretched anxiety I was feeling." I blink back tears and roll my shoulders to release some tension. "She told me that she didn't want to get married and that she didn't see a future with me. Finally, I heard the message that she had been trying to tell me. It was over. There was nothing I could do to change her mind." I wipe at my eyes and sigh.

"I feel for Qasida, but I also feel for you. You seem so kind, and it wasn't fair on you to manage all of this."

It was nice to hear someone else say it wasn't my fault. "I suppose so. I did a lot of bending, but I was at breaking point, and things couldn't have continued the way they were. She broke my heart, but she's still a very special person. I don't know if even she knows who she is. I think the family pressures, cultural expectations, and all of that overwhelmed her."

"Yes, it does appear that way. And what about you? Do you know who you are, what you want in life?" She checks her pocket watch again.

"I think I do now, more than ever. I'm still kind and compassionate, but I'm showing *myself* more compassion these days, and I'll never compromise on that again. I want to find someone new to share my affections with, but for now, I'm okay with just loving myself."

"That's a good way to look at things. I've always been consumed by my feelings for someone, but I think you're right. The love for oneself needs to come first."

"Absolutely." We smile at each other in mutual understanding. It felt incredible to be understood and to talk to someone so freely. For the first time in ages, I could breathe again.

I look down at my phone and see it's nearly midnight. Wow! Had we really been talking for this long? It had been such a thrilling and exciting evening, I can't quite believe it.

Anne stands and stretches her back slightly. "Laura, I would like to gift you my pocket watch. It's not much, and I have another at home. It would be an honour to me if you would keep it." Anne opens her pocket watch to show it to me. "Oh, goodness, it's almost midnight. The invitation said, 'Carriages at midnight,' so I think I shall need to leave soon." She snaps her pocket watch shut and gives it to me.

It's warm, and heavy, and comforting in my hand. "Wow, thank you so much. This is beautiful. Do you have to leave so soon? It's been an incredible evening." Though like any fairy tale, it has to come to an end.

She smiles and tenderly touches my cheek.

The clock chimes midnight and suddenly, Anne is gone. How did she go? Was she even here? *Laura, if you imagined this, you could imagine her back... Come on.* But how? I look outside. The road looks the same as always. A couple of cars drive past, and there's a man stumbling home from the pub, but apart from that, it's almost silent. I can hear the quiet hum of the motorway a couple of miles away.

My dream is over.

"Laura, are you joining us for cheese and biscuits? There's still a bit left for you. Unfortunately, all of the brie is gone but there's still some Applewood, which I know is your favourite." She stops and looks at me quizzically. "You were gone for ages. Is everything okay?"

"Oh, yes, sorry. Everything is fine," I say. I want to say no. No, I'd like to have another night, another time, another woman, but I will always remember this night.

As my parents and their friends chatter on and eat their supper, I feel a heavy weight in my pocket. I don't usually keep anything in there, and my phone is on the table. I reach inside and feel a cool, round, smooth object. As I pull it out of my pocket, I realise it's a pocket watch. Beautifully crafted with the Lister crest and motto, *Justus propositi tenax* meaning "Just and true of purpose," which I read about in her diaries. My heart beats hard against my chest. Could it be?

"What's that, love?"

"It's a pocket watch. I bought it last week," I answer. Mum would never believe what had happened this evening.

"Oh, Laura, you can never resist buying something once you set you heart on it, can you?"

"True." I smile, thinking once again of Anne. Her pride and courage to show the world who she truly was is awe-inspiring. Like her, I'm not prepared to change who I am for anyone. This is me, and I am enough.

Hostile

Saffron Sage

We have not seen each other for months.
I last reached out to you, and you didn't respond.
I let go. I begin to heal.
Our paths finally cross.
You are on a mission to regain your control over me.
You tell me I am hostile.
You tell me you can cut my hostility with a knife.
You don't know what those words mean.
I stand there in shock and see you with fresh eyes.
I see your malice and judgement towards me.
You instantly put my back up and I go into flight or fight mode.
I decide to fight my corner.
I tell you I am not hostile.
Hostile is such a strong word with so many connotations.
Hostile means showing feelings of opposition or dislike, unfriendly, antagonistic and aggressive.
I am none of those things.
Hostile means marked by malevolence, characteristic of an enemy, belligerent, and strongly rejecting.
I am none of those things.
What I am, I am because of the way you treated me.
But you can't see it. You think you're perfectly innocent.
Hostile.
Such a toxic word.
I thought our friendship was worth more than this.
I did not expect this from a friend.
But you're not a friend, are you? I've learned.
You are the hostile one in this relationship. Your words cut through me like a knife.
This can't be undone. I see you now.

Saffron Sage

You are a psychic vampire trying to suck all my energy away.
But my aura is bright and colourful like a rainbow and wraps around me to protect me from your vampirism.
My spiritual guides stand by me and protect me from your attack.
I am stronger than you think. I will not tolerate this.
I am worth more than this.
What a wonderful thing to know. To feel.
I walk away from you.
Not hostile. Not hurt. Not a victim.
Free.

People Tell You

Fern Wood

People tell you who you should be
By what you look like, how you dress
And what they want you to see

'Too ugly to be a girl and too plain to be a boy'
Your judgements always delivered with a smile
As you describe me as if I were a toy.

You told me who to love and how to feel
As if my story wasn't mine to tell
As if what I thought wasn't really real.

I changed my face, I changed my hair,
Thinking that would appease you,
But still I hear your voice, still I feel you there.

How do people work out who they are, how do they choose?
When each person tells you you're wrong, according to their rules
And there's always someone to lose?

I don't know who I am, and who I will be,
But I'm not just what you think,
I'm not just the person that you tell me to see.

As Far as I've Come

Vanessa Ball

24th June

Introductions

Hello and welcome. My name, the name I was given at birth and that has represented me for the thirty-four years of my life so far, is Lockwood.

It's a name that has come to mean so much to me and my connection to my family roots. Deep roots, that for a long time made me believe I had to present myself to the world in a way that was acceptable to those roots and my heritage. I feel my family name in every way, and yet there is another side to me that speaks of my own, unique self. A part that goes beyond the name and feels connected to life and newness. An acceptance of what has come before me, but what is also possible in the future.

Given half the chance to reflect on the journey you've been on with your own name, maybe you would come to the same conclusion. That we are our names but also so much more. The question is, how do we even begin to express our deepest selves when life is all-consuming and demands so much of us these days? Where do we even begin?

With a name. Lockwood. There's comfort to be found in those letters spoken together and out loud. When another speaks my name, I feel something similar to love. I'm wanted, needed, thought of by another. To speak my own name is special. I think of the history of our family. Our origins and those who came before me. To introduce myself to someone ignites a sense of wonder, because I have an ever-growing understanding of who I am and how I'm learning to interact with the world around me, but also because I'm intrigued by other people's perspectives. Of who they see when they first meet me and how that might change over time.

What's in a name? The answer. The whole of our Universe.

So, as I said before, my name is Lockwood, passed down to me by my loving parents, and their parents before them, and my great grandparents before them and beyond, into the distant past. And the Universe that willed me into existence. For what purpose, I'm still trying to discover.

But for now, I'd like to take this time to thank you for joining me on this journey of self-discovery through many stops, starts, and necessary mistakes made, more affectionately called life lessons, that have got me to where I am today. Much has changed for me in the past few months, and with change comes an opportunity to grow and feel that little bit more comfortable in the skin I occupy.

I've done a lot of growing up lately. You may not have suspected this once quiet and polite child, who would happily while away the hours in my own imagination, undisturbed and content, born into a family of strong characters who command any space they're in, would grow up to test the boundaries of their love. Rarely do we get a choice in the way life decides to carry us along. We're simply moved by the tides of time, and every now and then, something touches us and asks us to be honest with ourselves.

I always wanted to toe the line and make my family proud with my acceptable achievements. Go to school and learn. Tick. Attend a respectable university and obtain a degree. Tick. Meet a nice boy, settle down, and marry. Tick. The harshness of referring to those achievements as a tick box exercise should show you how I felt life had to be lived, trying to conform to the norm when there has never been anything normal about me. Other than the fact that I have the instinctive desire to feel safe, loved, and understood. Everything, or at least most of the rest of what makes up me, is unique only to me and my experiences.

Maybe who I am is dictated by the planets. Maybe the conversations I've had with myself and more recently with others about how I identify my capacity to love has shown me it was never a choice but a lesson in the acceptance of myself. To then share with others the importance of self-acceptance and compassion. To heal old wounds and finally nurture and love the inner child who was lost, and alone, and confused about how life could be lived and instead subscribing to a false idea of how it should be lived.

There are many avenues I could go down when trying to make sense of the journey I took to get from *one* understanding of myself to the *true* understanding of myself, but the clearest one is to reflect on those closest to me and the relationships that helped shape me.

As Far as I've Come

25th June
Mother

So, from where we left off yesterday, not that yesterday really matters anymore because we have the endless possibility of today, but for the purpose of this introduction, I must venture back in order to give you, dear reader, a better understanding and insight into my world. The experiences that have coloured my view of the world, the people I love and the lapse of time that has occurred since birth are my world.

Birth. My place of birth, London, and the individuals who came together to initiate my coming. The parents. My siblings. They all contributed to who I am today. So, I'll take this time to introduce them, one by one.

Mother was born and raised in Central America. Not to be confused with North or South America, but somewhere in between the two. Much of Mother's family eventually migrated to North America, and in particular, to New York City. A strong, independent, and fiercely loyal woman, Mother was born into a family of fourteen siblings. Being the eldest, she took on many of the responsibilities to help raise those siblings. Sadly, money wasn't a luxury afforded to my mother's family, but they had wealth far greater than anything money can buy. They had each other and the will to survive. This has the effect of building one's resilience in the face of adversity and enabled her to overcome difficulties with the strength of ten thousand warriors. My mother has always been my rock, my safe place, someone I can trust to always have my best interests at heart. I love her like no other, and I'm blessed to tell her that daily. If I'm ever in doubt of who I am and what I'm capable of, I turn to Mother, for her reassurance never falters.

Her life hasn't been an easy one, and her resolve to make a better life for her children has always been her goal. She's willed us to be kind to ourselves and never let the world tell us we are anything less than the blessings we are.

26th June
Father

I have introduced you to Mother. Now I bring into the ever-growing picture, my father, a man of both honour and very old, distorted views. That has and continues to bring me great anguish, but love surpasses even the most difficult qualities we find in each other.

We have a deep connection, an understanding of each other. I've taken the time to try and understand what makes his mind tick, why he does what he does and says, even when he knows it will upset others. Because as much as we are alike, we also couldn't be more different.

When I was a child, he treated me like a son. The only issue being that I have a vagina and am the youngest of four siblings, all the rest of whom are boys. So his doting on me and taking the time to impart his love and wisdom doesn't make much sense, but who am I to question the way life can turn out? If anything, that has been a blessing. Time spent with my father enriched my life and afforded me a wider perspective. My parents ensured I was never excluded from anything that could give me a fighting chance in the world.

Am I making much sense? Sometimes I struggle to verbalise my trail of thoughts into words that can be understood by others.

The most important thing to understand is that although my father grew up with old values, a lack of affection from his own family, and then spent many years in the army being conditioned not to show emotions, the love is there. It hides under layers of life experiences that shaped him and made him the man he is today.

I have no doubt about the love my father has for the family. He has always been there for me and never fails to come to my aid when I need him most. In return, I will always love him. For all the faults and poor ways of communicating with the world around him, he will always be my father and a good man.

1st July
Eldest Brother

The relationship between the eldest and youngest siblings is always, or at least traditionally, one of friction. I hesitate to say this because I'm sure, out there somewhere, there are successful stories of families who are capable of nurturing healthy, balanced relationships among all its members. But unfortunately, that wasn't the case within the complicated bonds of my family.

My experience with my older brother has always been one of frustration. We've struggled much of our lives to be kind to each other, always opting instead to be at loggerheads. The fact that we're so different in every way has a part to play in our difficulty to love and respect each other, but the fact that my brother is technically my half-brother may have played a part in the emotional barriers that created distance between us.

For the record, I've never seen him as anything but my older, bullying brother. I even got into a heated argument with my best friend at primary school when she tried to correct me about my own brother's status. *Half-brother*. There's nothing half about him. As far as I'm concerned, he was born out of our mother's womb and that makes us siblings. So, regardless of the fact that he spent the majority of my teen years teasing me about my suppressed sexuality, and regardless of the arguments, hurt feelings, and lack of real communication between us, I've learned to love him.

The years accumulated between us have softened us both and taught us to be kinder with our words. There is much to be appreciated and taken from some of the harsh lessons my eldest brother taught me. I'm grateful for those, as they have clued me in to the testing ways of the world in general and now that I'm more accepting of who I am, I can joke, "You were half right, brother."

4th July
Second Eldest Brother

"What's going on in that head of yours?" is a question we've always asked him. A quiet soul and never one to draw much attention to himself, he has always been a mystery to our close-knit, dysfunctional family unit.

He was quiet as a child, and this has followed him through to adulthood. We never shared much, other than nights out round the local town getting stupidly drunk whenever I came home from university.

We always worried about him. It was as if he had an internal battle that was too much to communicate to others. Instead of talking about what might have been going on, when he was old enough to hang out with friends—but still not old enough to legally drink—he started consuming copious amounts of alcohol. So excessive that Mother and Father would receive calls from his friends telling us that he was too drunk and needed saving. Later on, the drinking became more private, confined to the comfort of his own home and away from the suspicions of others who cared about him.

If someone were to ask me, "What do you know about your brother?" my honest answer would be not much at all really. Because that's just how things are. We're two very different people, with different expectations of life. He has his family, yearly holidays in the sun, and drinks by the fireside to keep him company. And he'll always have my love. Though I may never find the right time to tell him. Some things are just as they should be. We have a way of checking in with each other that doesn't require the normal formalities. We are forever bonded by a mother, father, and the sweeter memories of our childhood. So I carry on with life and will always wonder what goes on in my brother's head. I'll never get answers, but I've made my peace with that.

7th July
Twin Brother (by two years)

And now I come to my last brother. Where to begin with this tornado of energy and presence? My beloved brother and best friend.

An interesting fact, and one I always open with when I tell people about him, is that we were born on the same day, sharing one birthday, but exactly two years apart. Isn't that both amazing and strange? It never fails to make my head spin whenever I share this personal information with others, though no one but me ever seems blown away by this cosmic oddity. I follow this up with the classic, "I call myself his birthday present, and he's never stopped loving me."

With this insight, you might be able to imagine how close we've been over the years. Having spent much of our childhood moving from school to school, always the new kids, we learned very quickly to depend on each other, and in many ways, even as adults, we still support each other in whatever capacity time and distance allows. My love for my brother will never perish. Even when we are long gone and a faded memory to those who once knew us, we'll still have a connection.

He's the rebel of the family. He was the first to get into a fight at school and the first to really cause Mother and Father grief. He rebelled against authority and the world but never against me. If anything, thinking back on it now, he has always been loyal and respectful unless crossed by others in some way. And it's safe to say that it doesn't take a great deal to cross my dear, gung-ho brother. So there's been a lot to overcome and accept over the years. It's not been an easy ride for him, but it's been one full of life's lessons.

He received his hardest lesson at the age of thirty-five. Settled and with a family of four beautifully promising children and a devoted wife, my brother was diagnosed with stage four terminal cancer of the brain and given six months to live.

As a family, we're no strangers to cancer. Mother endured three bouts of it. She was able to overcome the physical and emotional trauma with admirable grace, determination, and the unrelenting love of her family.

My brother's cancer was nearly impossible to process and accept. I was shaken to my very core and prayed it wasn't true. But confirmation came, treatment began immediately, and fear ensued. This person I loved and had looked up to was going through the worst time of his life, and I didn't know what to do to make it better or how to help him through the nightmare that threatened his life and place in our world. I spent many mornings crying at the thought of losing him and the absence that would be created in my life. Evenings were spent feeling numb and trying to make sense of how this could have happened. A young, healthy man with the promise of a long life was about to be taken away from us.

With the help of those around me and a counsellor with a voice as soothing as warm honey dripped down a throat raw from all the wailing, I found a way through my own personal darkness and endeavoured to use what strength I had to bolster my brother and give him the positive encouragement needed when faced with such adversity. I knew he had the strength to fight this war and win. He comes from a family with such strong collective resolve that at times, I've felt carried through my own difficulties by it.

Winning this battle is being achieved on a daily basis. The doctors gave him six months, but he smashed through that declaration with the greatest hammer of hope. Almost a year and a half later, he's still here, teaching us that love and determination conquer all difficulties in life and that miracles really do happen.

8th July
Coming Up and Out

So here we are. We've come full circle back to me and a snapshot of a monumental turning point in my life: the acceptance of myself and the sharing of this acceptance with my beloved family.

The day(s) I came out to my family were the most liberating of my life. No words can truly do justice to what I felt then and thereafter, but maybe the closest to it is euphoric. The complete acceptance of myself and what

I believe to be true of my authentic nature gave me a sense of euphoria. The word itself is beautiful and my feelings matched that.

That's not to say there wasn't fear and panic leading up to that moment, but there was so little time between knowing my truth and needing to share it after years of suppression and denial, that I couldn't keep it to myself. I needed the ones I loved to be with me in whatever capacity they were willing and able to accept.

Mother was the first to find out. I believe having given birth to me, she had a claim on this entitlement. One morning, while I sat outside with my morning journal, I knew the time was right. I walked into the kitchen of my parents' home and found Mother where she loved to be, cooking delicious food to remember her homeland and to nourish her family.

I took a deep breath and let the words come forth any which way they chose to. Part of my fear was that my mother and best friend of thirty-four years would reject me out of shame. This fear came from a misguided understanding that it went against her cultural and religious beliefs, but I was forgetting something crucially important. She was a woman who fiercely loved her children and would fight tooth and nail to see us through any situation, deemed good or bad, in our lives.

In tears, I told her I was queer, and the response I received was a testament to my mother's enduring love. She embraced me and told me that whatever choices I made in life, she would always be by my side and would never stop loving me. I let myself go in her arms and cried tears of relief. The woman I admired for all her strength and wisdom hadn't turned her back on me. She'd accepted me for who I am. No questions asked. A simple understanding shared between mother and daughter that our bond could never be broken.

Next was Father. This declaration of my queerness was completely spontaneous and rather abrupt. My father, as stated, is a wonderful man who has always supported his wife and children. He is the archetype of the hero. He served most of his life in the armed forces and provided us with a safe environment to grow up in. We never had to struggle for physical and emotional comforts. And as the only girl of four children, I was never excluded from anything that may have been deemed too masculine for a girl. My father has always happily regaled me with tales about army life and had me muck in with the more physical chores around the house and garden. That helped me to embrace both my feminine and masculine qualities.

The coming out in question came when I was sat at the dining room table at my parents' home, enjoying my mother's cooking and general conversation. The radio was playing quietly in the background as we chatted but was just loud enough to be heard when Frankie Goes to Hollywood came on.

"Gays," was my father's instant response.

My automatic counter response was, "Your daughter is gay."

Well, I knew I would eventually find the right time to tell him, but Father was trickier than the others, and I had originally thought it would take a little more time and planning, but with all the best intentions, plans can and will only take you so far. Intention and opportunity will carry you the rest of the way.

After a moment's reflection and digestion of this hot-tempered delivery of news, my father came back with a very surprising, but very male, response.

"Well, as long as the woman you bring back is as pretty as you."

This was my father's sweet but backwards way of showing his acceptance. He grew up with distorted views about the LGBT+ community, and even with all my efforts to correct him, I thought I would have more of a battle on my hands. But our fears can grow out of proportion, and the expectations we have of others can also become distorted by that very same fear.

Later, he told me to be careful about joining groups or marches for fear that I would put myself in the way of danger, but I reassured him that times were changing and even though that's still a possibility, you have to stand up for what you believe in, even in the face of adversity. My father's love has never wavered.

The revelation to my brother came when a golden opportunity presented itself. You have to take these opportunities when they appear, and take this one I did, with an ever-growing sense of pride in who I am and a receding fear of what people may think of me.

With the eldest brother, a joke was shared. Maybe the fact that I never confirmed or denied his accusations was a big tell, but even I didn't know myself back then, so I can be forgiven for taking my time.

I'm not completely sure if my second to eldest brother was ever officially informed by me or anyone else, but I'm sure he's aware now. In the flurry of exchanged words and the constant coming and going from the family hub, he may have been overlooked, but be reassured he's a quiet soul and as deep as any well. Just the knowledge that you're okay and getting on with life is enough to keep him content that he doesn't need to step in and defend anyone's honour.

My self-appointed twin was told on a flying visit through the parents' home. I knew it wouldn't be much longer until something was said in passing, and my love and respect for him also informed how and when I shared my news. I didn't want to cause him any upset, as his circumstances made us all very protective of him, but this was a truth that I couldn't deny myself or him. I told him of my new-found acceptance and gave him a reassuring smile—everything was going to be okay, and although my life was going through some major shifts, this was a truth that would help me heal and find my way back to myself and my own happiness.

Over the past few months, it's been something he has gradually come to terms with, after telling me on a number of occasions that it's just a phase I'm going through. The reality of my truth has settled with him. I knew he would struggle to accept my revelation, but I also knew that this was something I had to do for my own well-being, regardless of the possible fallout. To have his love and acceptance makes a world of difference to my happiness. He'll always be my twin, and our bond has only strengthened through the challenges we've all faced together, as a family.

So, this is the story of how my family embraced me for who I am and have always really been. I hope that sharing my story will help you find courage to speak your truth, because when you learn to believe in yourself and what you stand for, others won't be far behind.

Much love always,
Sophia.

The Journey
Saffron Sage

I FIRST QUESTIONED MY sexuality at sixteen. Am I straight, bi, or gay? I didn't know. Subconsciously, I liked girls, but I tried to keep up with the norm and date boys. I never got the emotional connection with boys, and I always questioned why it never felt quite right. It always felt like I was this person trying to make it normal, but I felt like an imposter in the relationship. I was trying to live up to the expectations of my family to have a nice boyfriend. I decided at eighteen that I was bi, and I started going to gay bars and meeting girls but also continued dating boys. The first time I went to a gay bar was like going to a different planet and seeing the world with different eyes. I felt excited by being in a place I could express myself without any judgement from others. I had butterflies, but this was my happy place where I could be myself and be free. I met people on my wavelength who understood where I was coming from. My first Gay Pride march was an amazing, electric experience... the noise, the flags, the colours, the happiness, the freedom to be who you wanted to be. I kissed a girl for the first time. I will never forget my first kiss, and that was the start of my journey.

I kept this side of my life hidden from my family and tried to express my sexuality and explore my feelings and emotions on my own. It was a lonely part of my life, but I met other people who were experiencing similar times and made good friends who are still part of my life now. At twenty-one, I came out as a lesbian to my nan. She was my rock and my confidante. She told me that as long as it made me happy, I should go with my feelings. My nan was a very spiritual lady, born in the wrong times. She liked crystals, herbs, and alternative therapies and was connected to God. For a Welsh sheep farmer's wife, she was not the norm. She didn't judge me for exploring my sexuality, and she encouraged me to explore who I was and who I wanted to be. When she met my gay male friends, she said, "They're nice boys." Not what I expected. She even questioned her opinion of gay men and was more embracing of the gay community, which made me smile.

Even though Nan is now in spirit, I still feel her presence with me a lot and when I see white feathers, I associate them with an angelic sign of her. I see the feathers as a message that she's still with me now. I can sense her spirit around me, and it's usually at a time in my life when I need a sign or when I'm seeking a spiritual connection. She's always with me when I use my crystals, and Reiki, and when using angelic symbols. I miss her wise words and support a lot, especially when I'm at a crossroads, as I was several years ago.

I remember sitting alone on the beach early in the morning, meditating and asking Buddha for a sign to show me how to change my life. I hadn't been happy for a while and had been in a toxic relationship. I'd been feeling lonely and lost, and I knew that there must be more to my life than what I had. I sat on the quiet, empty beach, picking up shells and asking the Universe and my female spiritual guide to please show me the way. Amazingly, the sign came in the form of a pod of dolphins swimming in the bay. The dolphins symbolised freedom and being carefree, which is how I wanted to feel in my life. It made me smile, and I made my mind up then and there as I'm a great believer in signs, karma, and messages. I made the huge decision to walk away from my long-term relationship, to start anew, and to find myself again. I had lost my way looking after someone else's needs and their aspirations, which no longer felt like part of my path. But where to start? I wanted my own inspirations and life goals to do what I wanted to do in my life. I wanted to feel alive again, feel excited about life, and be loved and nurtured once more. I wanted to feel fulfilled and happy again.

Little did I know that destiny was already in motion, and I'd already met my soulmate. Our paths had crossed a few times already. She has a dolphin tattoo on her arm and is my divine serendipity. This had been the main crossroad in my life. I'd moved forward, and I know I can be truly loved, wanted, and needed by an amazing partner who's on my wavelength. This time of change made me feel settled and happier in myself. I could express how I really felt, and I know that I can trust my instincts in seeing signs from the Universe. I no longer felt I was chasing rainbows and that I could trust in my spiritual connections. I encourage others to take notice of signs, karma, and spiritual connections as they come at a time in your life as a divine intervention when you're least expecting them.

My mum has been on her own journey in taking time to accept my life choices and decisions. She has embraced my partner and treats her like her own daughter, which is wonderful. Mum lets her take over her kitchen and teach her how to cook. She encourages my creative side, my alternative therapy interests, and my spirituality. She's quite spiritual in her own way and believes in white feathers as a sign too. Mum is my wise owl and gives good advice whether I want to hear it or not. She always tells the truth, which I respect. My partner sees my mum as a surrogate mother too, which I love. I'm very lucky to have such an accepting mum.

I now look back on my life and see the sixteen-year-old me being unsure, questioning, and curious about her sexuality. My heart aches for her. I'd like to tell her to keep exploring her sexuality and choices, and to carry on making those mistakes in life in order to get to a place of happiness, until she feels the freedom to do what she wants so she can feel loved. I have evolved since then, and my confidence in my sexuality has developed throughout my life experiences.

It's been a hell of a personal journey with lots of ups and downs. I no longer need to question myself or my choices. I'm finally happy and feel I can be my true, authentic self. I can be out and proud as a lesbian woman, and I can embrace *not* being the norm.

Finite Forgiveness

AP Bramley

If you wonder why some people
Will get forgiveness a thousand times
And others won't get forgiven once
The answer is very simple.

See, I know the difference
Between those who try
And those who don't.
I know those who are growing
and learning with me
For me
Because of me.

And they will be forgiven
For every mistake, every slip up
Because their apologies are marked
With love and care
Braced on questions about me
About my comfort
About the things that hurt
And the things that help.
They are willing to rewrite language
learned over a lifetime
To make sure I feel at home.

There are others who don't compare
Whose apologies are marred with excuses
For why learning a new language is so difficult
As if I haven't heard it all before
As if I don't know that you're trying to justify your behaviour

Pinning the weight of your mistakes
on my shoulders
By expecting me to be
the understanding one
The forgiving one
The patient one
The one who needs to adapt for you
Who needs to wait for you.
You will find my forgiveness in short supply
Until you can prove to me
That you've earned it.

Out and Proud

Andrea (Annie) Alleyne

Out and Proud, out and proud... that's what I'm supposed to be!
Out and Proud, out and proud but what if that just isn't me?
Does that mean I'm ostracised, outcast, and shut out?
Does it mean I can't be proud unless I'm prepared to shout?

Can I be me? Can I be proud and live a quiet life?
Can I be me? Can I be proud and live a life implied?
Not everyone wants to live their lives under bright, hot spotlights,
Not everyone wants to march at Pride, wave a flag, and fight for Our rights.

Some people want a quiet life without torment, torture, and drama.
Is it possible to just live day by day doing good deeds, inviting good karma?
Not everyone is daring, and bold, and ready to put themselves on show,
Not everyone has a community behind them or somewhere safe to go.

Some people like the quiet life, they like to slip under the radar.
Does it mean I'm only worthy of acceptance if I'm an activist or a crusader?
Can I be loved? Can I be included without having to come out?
Or will my lack of visibility call my authenticity into doubt?

So many issues to overcome for someone who's Black, and Female, and Gay!
So many causes to support in life, but who's supporting me?
I'm out and proud, in my own way... understated but not defined.
I'm out and proud, in my own way... living a life of my own design.

I'm out, and I'm proud, and I'm brave every day, without being on the front lines.

Tits

Sara Gray

THIS STORY IS ALL about tits. It begins with tits, (well, at least for me) and it ends with tits, (well, because of them, at least). I'm not talking about the cute, fluffy flying tits which grace our hedgerows at the first hint of spring with their shrill chirrups and beaks stuffed with hope and moss. Just to be clear and to avoid any ambiguity, I'm speaking of human, female breasts. The bosoms, the mammary, the boobs, the jugs, or whatever it is you like to call them. For me, it has always been tits.

It begins with tits purely because they were there with me when the first signs of being different began to show. In fact, I was like no one else I knew after my initial encounter with my sapphic leanings. I can even see them now.

I remember feeling the burn in the air from the sun as it baked the little lean-to conservatory and made everything inside it dry up. Each item had faded, curled, or turned brown. It felt like another world. A world of has-been and crispy, dusty clutter and wonder. A den where you were almost invisible if you breathed quietly enough. I had to be invisible, and yet I knew deep down that I was glaringly obvious, out of place, almost out of time. But I felt like another me in there, sitting on a dusty, green cut-off carpet. Bits of cat litter dug into my crossed ankles. My left ankle bone scraped on bare concrete. The stench of a cat litter box mingled with cat food to inform every intruder that this wasn't a human zone. But it was my favourite place in the whole wide world. Especially since last night.

On my left is a box, in front of me is a ramshackle pile of papers already beginning to curl under the sun's onslaught of constant heat. To my right is the offending litter tray. I peer over the edge of the box, inching my neck so that my chin barely rises over the rough corrugated ridge, my heart pounding in my chest, my temples, my wrists. I'm stretching almost beyond the limit of gravity when I catch sight of the squirming contents. My heart leaps out of my chest, and I am transmogrified as I simply stare, barely even breathing. I'm vaguely aware that I'm on a precipice of sheer bliss, all other senses dulled by the wonderful sight of brand-new kittens nuzzling their tired-looking mum. I know I'm not allowed in here. I have been expressly forbidden entry, yet this box holds such fascination, and I can't hold back my defiance. If She catches me, I'm dead. But She won't know. She is in bed, as usual. Five little chests rise and fall, five tiny tails, tiny toes kneading happily on various sets of paws, and one very pissed off cat, green eyes staring straight at me, tail flicking in annoyance. Not even my bright smile is appeasing her.

"Saraaaa!"

Shit. Shit, shit, shit, shit, shit! I try to edge back gently, try to get up silently, try to feel sensation beyond the numbness in my limbs. I catch my knee on a hard pebble of cat litter. I wince, lurch sideways and grab onto the pile of papers only to flounder even more as my handful dislodges the pile, sending the stack spewing everywhere. A plant pot spills its muck onto the already soiled floor and refuses to go away despite my frantic hand-sweeping.

"Sara!"

Shit, shit, shit! I'm done for. I'm never going to get away with this now. I frantically plead with Fluffy, using my telepathic powers, and beg her not to grass me up. I hastily scoop the disarray of old newspapers together and replace them on top of the remaining pile. I attempt my stealthy return to the land of the living only to be greeted in the kitchen by an even bigger set of eyes bearing down on me. An even more pissed off mother is behind them. This time, it's mine.

Hot tears are still streaming down my face and over the swollen red slap marks on my cheek when She drives off. I hate her so much right now. My face really hurts but worse than that, she's gone without me. I'm not being allowed to go food shopping as punishment. Not fair! I'll have to wait yet another week until I get to browse the stationery aisle, to gorge on the freshly stacked pads of paper and packets of crisp, pointed pencils that I'll never possess. My one and only bliss is staring at pens, pads, stickers, rubbers, pencils, and colouring books. I love to leaf through a brand-new colouring book and look at the same pictures over and over. The puppies and kittens in cartoon form, heavy black lines bending and sweeping over the pages, making up rules of their own. I like to look for my favourite picture of what I believe is a beautiful palace with tall columns topped with multi-faceted and curved roof tops, each one with a different set of swirls or line patterns to colour in. I always save this picture until last in a new book, each time aiming to stay inside the lines on every tiny section. Until just a few moments ago, I would long for this trip to the shop more than anything else in a whole week.

I could go back downstairs though, see the kittens. Dare I come out of my room? She thinks I'm going to stay here on my bed as per the Commandment to Honour thy father and thy mother. Well, she can think again. Stuff it! I'm going back in. I *need* to go back in. Fluffy might have been scared by all of the screaming and all of those slaps. I need to make sure she's okay. And I have to see the kittens again. I have to make sure that they're still there. I might not be allowed out for a very long time. I count to ten, peer out of my window to make doubly, triply sure the car is gone.

Reassuringly, pale concrete lies beneath my bedroom window, and there is no hint of the blue Mini. Still, I slide my legs over the edge of my bed and silently lower my feet onto the floor. I creep across an only slightly cleaner green carpet than the one in the conservatory and stand by my door handle. *Breathe silently, Sara. Stop your stupid crying, Sara. Don't let Her see She upset you.* Such a well-practiced routine of creeping around. Being invisible. I'm good at this now.

I go back to the conservatory. I might not have much time, and I absolutely must not be discovered this time. She might get rid of them if I am. Fluffy is almost sleeping on this visit. I desperately want to pick her up, bury my face into her piles of long black hair, and tell her how sad I am, but something tells me to leave her alone. I decide to stay on my feet. Safer. Easier to run the second I hear the car coming up the drive. The kittens aren't doing much anyway.

My gaze is drawn to that huge pile of papers which had given me away earlier. The top one has big letters on it saying something about someone called Argie, and there's a picture of Lady Di kissing Prince Charles. It makes me squirm a bit, because I can't imagine anything more gross than kissing. Yuck! We've only just been given this pile of papers. Something to do with needing them for the kittens. The puppies are going to be born any day now too, apparently, and we'll need lots of it then, so She has been to all of the neighbours for papers. I turn the top page over, if anything just so I can stop seeing that disgusting snogging. Even the best description of how I felt when I saw what was on the next page will never come close to what it was like to be little nine-year-old me in that moment.

There, smiling like I was giving her the best day of her life, was a woman with absolutely nothing on. I knew immediately that she should have had *everything* on, but for some reason she was just there, naked! Her shoulders, her chest, her belly button, her bum, her thighs, her...well, she had pants on, at least. Her tits! I can see her tits! My stomach flipped over and sat high up in my throat, but not in an "I'm going to be sick" way. This was something else. I felt a bit sweaty and dizzy. I couldn't smell the cat piss or feel the sun anymore. Gone was the gravel on my heels, and all I could feel was this slightly painful heat somewhere in a place inside of me that I didn't know I had. I couldn't stop staring.

She was beautiful. She made *me* feel beautiful. She made me feel like I was supposed to be there looking at her. There was a little story about her too. Her name, some numbers (I thought that might have been her phone number) what she liked to do, that sort of thing. *I can see her tits!* Apparently, you've got to keep coming back to see her again soon. Could there be more? I look over to the pile of papers. It's almost as tall as I am. Could there really be more of this? I'm not sure that I want or need to close this current encounter but, as the saying goes, curiosity killed the cat, and I've clearly got nine lives if the events from earlier are a behavioural barometer.

I stare at the next paper on the pile. Something about a boat being sunk. I know it's about a war. The war scares me, and I know only too well that soldiers don't always come home. My daddy didn't come home six years ago. What if she's there again? I turn the front page back. Each micro movement from my shaky little hand creates a cacophony of cracks and crackles as the reluctant, compressed paper remembers how to bend. I feel as though I'm breathing through jelly, caught somewhere between ability and paralysis as I slowly reveal the next page. And slowly, I find to my utter delight that there is indeed another photograph of another naked lady smiling straight at me. My world is suspended like a party balloon as I take in another set of curves, study another flawless face framed by voluminous curls, and really shiny lips and eyelids. Now I'm staring at her tits. And I'm getting that funny feeling again. These tits are different to the first ones. They're darker in the middle, and her nipples are smaller. I think I like them better, and now I want to look at every page number 3 of every paper in this huge pile.

I don't how much longer I stayed and stared that day, but I'll never forget the euphoria in those moments of sheer beauty. Over the coming days, I couldn't wait to have the house to myself so that I could go and look again. Always the same dizzy feeling, always the same flippy tummy, and always that funny little pain. I'd feign disinterest at going shopping, fake illness to skip school and be able to steal precious minutes when She was taking my brother to school. Any chance I got, I was in there. Sometimes, on a weekend, She would be in her sewing room. You weren't allowed in there, and She would be in there for the whole day, so we could go anywhere else in the house, and She wouldn't know about it. And the papers just kept arriving. My den had developed into a whole new dimension. I didn't know it at the time, but I would spend a great deal of my future travelling back and forth between two worlds, always preferring this two-dimensional utopia.

I spent the whole summer offering to help out with the kittens and the puppies. Especially the puppies. They needed a lot of papers and several times per day. I remember finding out that I was the only person who absolutely loved looking for the third page. She pretended it wasn't there, my little brother giggled the first few times but got bored, and my best friend just pulled a funny face. All the more for me then.

I longed to grow tits of my own. If I had tits, I'd be happy just like those women were. I remember sitting on the loo, legs swinging far from the floor, clasping my hands together in earnest and praying to God for big tits when I grew up. That day, in a way, was day one of coming out to myself. Of course, I didn't know it at the time, and I certainly didn't have the words, and it would be many years until I did. As a result, I have been in and out of the closet more times than a left leg doing the hokey cokey.

It is somewhat of a cliché, the lesbian surrounded by cats. I began my journey into discovering what I am when I was surrounded by cats. I tell people (mostly straight people who need an extra level of explanation) that I knew I was into women from that moment. I didn't know what that was then, had never heard of the words I came to learn and embrace. It would be a very long time until I did.

It would be four more years and a house move until my next world-shattering moment of knowing something was different about me. By this time, I know about gays (I grew into a teenager during the AIDS epidemic and can still remember that infamous tombstone leaflet and those adverts on the telly). I knew I was one. I just wasn't allowed to *be* one. God would basically wipe me off the face of the Earth if I even thought about tits too much, according to Her and the world around me. It didn't stop me though, and now I had even more material for my lascivious deviations. Music videos beamed all kinds of sexual deviancy right into my living room. NME. Madonna. Cyndi Lauper. And oh, good God, Chrissie Hynde. But no, none of them were meant for me. One day, I'd have a nice, clean-living virgin, a God-fearing husband. Oh God. I tried harder not to think about tits. But I've read about sex as a necessity in my 11-13 biology book. AND THERE IS NO FUCKING WAY THAT'S GOING IN ME. EVER.

I become weirdly fascinated by someone who didn't even know I existed. She lived across the road from my house, and uphill a bit, sort of around the bend. I caught sight of her one day when I was prancing about in front of my mirror trying to look like I know how to dance on *Top of the Pops,* just in case I ever got to go there. (Fat chance. Pop music is being masterminded by the Devil). The moment I saw her, I almost chinned myself on my bedroom heater by ducking down in case she happened to be watching me too. When I was brave enough to peer over the windowsill again, she was walking straight towards our house (Shit!) but then veered off onto the park. She was with another woman who was a skinhead (really scary), and they had quite a few dogs.

And I just *knew* that we were the same. Except that she was the grown-up version of me. And way cooler. So, so, so cool. So tall, so thin, so everything in her black top, and skin-tight black jeans, and jet-black hair, all spiky and black shades, and bright red lips. Look at how she walks! *So cool.*

I stared and stared until they were out of sight. Something about them, something about how close together they walked, looked at each other, smiled, made me believe that they were what I had recently learned about. Dykes. I needed to follow them, wanted to watch them embrace and snog behind a tree in the fields while the dogs had their walk, wanted them to wave and say hello. No, definitely not that! But I was convinced that if I did follow them, I would absolutely get to see them snogging. Why else would they be going for a dog walk together into the fields? I had to find an excuse to follow them. Get them to notice me and feel an equal amount of curiosity about me. Most importantly, I needed them to know that I was one of them. One of what, exactly? The Cool People of the Cool Clothes Club? I thought about my school uniform and my church clothes and rued the day that I had pleaded for snow-washed denim. It had to be black now. *Guess I'm not going anywhere soon.* The reality of my uncool prison descended like a muggy damp cloud with weights on it. I'd have to content myself with just catching a glimpse of them as and when I could, even if that meant constantly staring up the road at their flat at every given opportunity. I desperately needed to see them snogging though.

I worked out that I had precisely fifteen seconds from seeing them leave their flat in order to grab a dog from our pack, clip a lead to it, announce the reason for my sudden departure from the house, and leg it out of the front door to then nonchalantly stroll down the drive and into the park at the same time as they did to be in with a chance of seeing them in person. All of the gear and no idea. On the last two occasions I'd tried this strategy, She had other ideas about what I should be doing instead. One time, I had to set the table and the other time I hadn't tidied my room. How did She even know? She hadn't been near my room all day. I was just so sick of being told what to do. Next time, I wouldn't ask, I would just go. Sod the dog, sod the repercussions, sod everything. As a strategy to get out of the house, it worked. In terms of having my curiosities satisfied, I was bitterly disappointed. There was no snogging. No hand-holding. No music video moments of lingering looks or desperate embracing. They just walked the dogs. I was bitterly disappointed.

One day, the really tall woman stopped and started walking back up the path towards me. So tall, so skinny, oh my God, her jet-black hair was so, so cool! I bet she was from London and had been to all of the cool clubs I'd read about in my friend's magazines, and now she was walking straight towards me. Say something! What do I say? She got to me before I had the half a day needed to create a meaningful encounter, and I simply stepped sideways, almost in tears of awe.

She smiled and just said, "Ta, duck."

In my head, she kept talking. *Yes, I too have been dying to meet you. I see you standing at the top of your drive three times per week, in your square-bear church clothes waiting for your mum to reverse the car up, and I've seen your little brother in his little two-piece suit with his little briefcase. Can I come round? And will you read the Bible to me? Do you want to leave home and move in with me and my girlfriend?* And then she was out of sight.

How had that gone so wrong? I fucking hated myself. I turned, giving up on everything right then and there, and went home. I opened the closet, stepped inside, and sat down on top of the old fusty slippers and floppy topped winter boots. I shut the door and lamented that I was in a state somewhere between Job and Nebuchadnezzar and eternal bleakness.

I wrote in my journal, ages later when I was thinking of that time in my life:

You never stopped fascinating me. I always watched you coming and going, but you outranked me in so many ways. Your swagger, and your grown-upness, and all the other side stories that I invented for you over the next three years. Sometimes I would notice that you were watching telly in the dark. The tell-tale blue haze flickering on and off in your window. I would try and guess what you were watching, and I would turn the dial through the stations of my tiny black and white portable to see if I could guess what it was you'd be drawn to. You've been into my house, made friends with my mum, probably heard all about what a little shit I am and how much of a child I am. I would hide when you were here, unable to face you. I need to get out of this shit hole and into your kind of lifestyle. I don't want to be with you, I'm not trying to be you…well, maybe a bit. I just know that you're the only person for a hundred miles that's like me. Make that three hundred miles. I know you'll never in a million years know this side of me or know what I think about. And what I think is irrelevant anyway, because God is never ever going to suddenly change his mind about dykes or poofs. We're all doomed.

I left all that theological guilt behind me the day that I rode off, aged sixteen, on Carl's motorbike, wearing a borrowed leather jacket and helmet. And I came back a year later, this time on my own motorbike and with my own helmet. I wondered if you were still there. Had you even realised I'd gone? I revved my bike at the top of the drive and took the long way out of the estate to speed past your flat. It was your turn to notice me being cool. I had edge now. I was officially what was known as a "Tit-Biker." I played my metal and heavy rock at full volume as often as possible. I needed everyone to know that I was officially disassociated with the God-fearing lifestyle, and I came and I went, just as I pleased. Well, almost. I was old enough, strong enough, that She could no longer intimidate me. I didn't have to be afraid. I was learning myself like a book being written a line at a time.

The day that we met properly ultimately created a memory for us to reminisce upon over and over again for the next thirty-plus years and find it somehow funnier each time we relived it.

I was cat-sitting for my mum, but I'd forgot my keys and had to gain entry through the open kitchen window. I had my hands planted on the edge of the kitchen sink, my stiletto-booted feet were flying at half-mast in the air, my hips were painfully pinned to the windowsill, and my leather jacket was wedged in the space between my arse and the edge of the open window. Suddenly, there was a force applied to the back of my jeans, and the past ten minutes of excruciating progress into the kitchen were erased in a millisecond.

"Oi! What the fuck do you think you're doing?" A gruff voice rang out of the blackness.

And then a softer, more hesitant voice said, "Leave it, Luce, leave it."

"Get the fuck off me, you twat! I live here!" My feet skidded like Bambi on the wet concrete, almost snapping my ankles as I hastily rearranged my skewed clothes, shoved my tits back into my V-neck, and attempted to part my huge, bushy head of hair in order to see my assailant.

"Luce, it's Zara. Zara, is that you?"

I knew that voice. I was simply mortified. I didn't fucking believe it. And I used to be bothered by snow-washed jeans not being cool? How about being pulled ass first out the window of your own house?

"I don't care, Jeanette. What the fuck is going on?"

"It's okay," I somehow managed to pant. "I forgot my key. I was trying to get in to feed the cats."

Luce looked at me with more scepticism than a Labour voter at a Tory Party Conference. Something in what Jeanette says to her sank in. I didn't have my fighting head on and even if I had, I doubted that I would ever stand a chance against such a well-built, well-centred, well-meaning lezza. I noticed that Jeanette looked more amused than bemused. Her tall silhouette was framed in the street lighting, her hair jet black against the orange glow, and her (huge!) hands gripped tightly to one end of a lead, which stopped at the neck of the biggest Doberman Pinscher I had ever seen.

"She's all rayt. She'll not hurt ya."

I took that as a cue to fuss the dog. I had no idea if this was all happening at the pre- or post-snogging in the field excursion that I was still convinced *must* happen at some point, but in that moment, I didn't even equal the level of cool I hadn't possess in 1986. *Please God, don't say stupid things. Don't ask them in for a cup of tea and a church biscuit...*

"Duck, do you need our key?" Luce looked directly at me.

"Erm, yeah, please. That would be much easier, thank you."

I'd made it! That was my invite! Oh, I was off to Nirvana and into the Flat of Wonder. Luce just shoved her hand into her jeans and twisted off a useful sliver of metal in two smooth movements.

"Thanks." I hoped my bitterly disappointed gratitude wasn't taken for sullenness.

"How's yer mam?"

Jeanette seemed happy to stand and natter, and yet I really didn't want to be there in this totally ruined moment and make chit-chat about Her! "Yeah, good thanks. Right, I better be off. Thanks for the key. I'll bring mine tomorrow and drop yours off."

Jeanette looked down the drive. "That your bike?"

"Yeah, it is. Do you like bikes?"

"I used to have one years ago. Wouldn't get me on one now. We've seen you loads on it. I said to Luce, I think that's Zara."

You knew my name! You DID see me! You DID know I existed all those years! Could you smell the lesbianism on me like I could on you? Of course you couldn't. I hadn't got a girlfriend or a field to snog her in. I was so deeply in awe that you even knew that I existed that I didn't correct your pronunciation of my name. And I never would. And you called me Zara from that moment on. I wanted to tell you that I'd finally made it out. I wanted to tell you that I still adored tits. I wanted to tell you that I was an almost visitor to L'Amour in town, and that I once accidentally walked into The New Foresters, shit myself, and walked out again, and regretted it instantly. I wanted to ask you how I could start to be a real lesbian. But I didn't. You ambled back to your perfect dimension with your girlfriend and your dog, and I turned the key in the door and found myself surrounded yet again by an empty house, and an avalanche of cats, and a sense of almost made it. At least I'd grown my own tits now—some prayers do get answered.

I was in my early thirties when that left hokey cokey leg finally landed firmly on out. And you were there as my constant mentor, my very best friend, and rock-steady ally. We had bumped into each other just after my divorce from my husband, after my ex-communication from the Church, and right in the middle of my favourite years of being a mum. I was determined to make that decade about being true to who I was, mentally, physically, spiritually, and to make something of myself and embrace my sapphic origins. You charmed the tits off everyone in every venue we ever went in. It helped massively that you could be seen from every vantage point in any bar or club, you being so very tall and so striking to look at. Your style never changed, your manner never changed, people from your life thirty years prior would seek you out for a catch-up.

I was your little tag-along, and you allowed me to study your craft and watch you in action. We would talk for hours, walk your Dobermans for hours (actually, it was more you talking to everyone and anyone we met along the way), and ruminate over fancying, loving, and leaving women for hours. And I would spend hours wiping your red lipstick off everything and anything you touched. Your red lips and your name were synonymous to anyone within a three-foot radius of you. The only present you ever asked for was red lippy. You were the bearer of gifts to all your friends and lovers, always hunting out a specially chosen bargain in a charity shop, always one step ahead of the recipient in knowing what they wanted. And you're rarely wrong.

I have always told everyone that you guided me through some of my biggest and most life-defining decisions. From being the thirteen-year-old wannabe stalker to feeling safe coming out, speaking to my family, supporting me with raising my kids, and making them feel whole and loved. You became Aunty Netty. And they, like little me, thought you were so cool with your ever-increasing tattoo collection and Converse trainers. Like the day you arrived with a full-on fish tank filled with fish and a Doberman puppy just as I was getting my mental head on to shoo three children into their school uniforms. You had sleepovers for them and shopping excursions to find bargains or to return three-day old purchases to IKEA because you'd changed your mind again. Your ability to talk the hind leg from a donkey was coupled with an insatiable need to be constantly reinventing your homes and their contents. A woman who never stopped unless you were felled by the depression, which at times would take over and sap you of your energy.

There was a phone call one day.

"Can you come over?"

You never asked me to do that. I dropped the kids off and found you with an ashen look, matched by an edge that I could feel the moment I walked into your home.

"I need you to help me, Zara. Dog will need looking after too, probably next week or week after."

Okay. And? I nodded and gave her a quizzical look.

"I've got a lump. Think I've got to have me tit off."

There was no room big enough in that moment to prevent the walls from closing in after that statement. It was as though a force had sucked every atom from the room, and from my lungs, and from my brain.

"Jeanette," was all I could muster.

"Be rayt, Zara. Told him I just want it off. Not pissin' about wi' it."

I drove to your hospital bedside with your then girlfriend, cradling a strawberry McFlurry. You saw us enter the ward and immediately asked the nurse to pass you your red lippy. Everyone laughed and marvelled at your need to project super-cool even at your most vulnerable.

Within a week of having your first mastectomy and your lymph nodes removed, the biopsy from your remaining breast indicated a second mastectomy was recommended. This one didn't have the same pea-sized lump as the first, but it was full to the brim with bad cells. I was so angry at your tits, so afraid that their absence would leave you feeling like your life was over. I wanted to jump into your space at times and give you my head, and let you feel just how much love was there for you and how strong and enduring our friendship was. You would not have to deal with any of this alone.

And you recovered.

And we clocked up many more hours of chewing the fat. Doing stupid things, meeting different people, learning all about the internet and its dating highs and pitfalls. That certainly opened up a whole new world.

I think I created something like twenty different profiles, and logins, and email addresses for you, as one by one you forgot them all! You once gave me a book entitled *Abnormal Psychology,* which piqued my interest in mental health. You'd spoken to me about your own mental health and a brush with psychosis as a younger woman. I devoured it. That led to me ending my career as a business consultant and going for gold with a fresh degree in psychology. You introduced me to your ex, we hit it off, flopped, and then I met her ex, and a sixteen-year relationship followed that. Meanwhile, you had to go through a few more break-ups before you found your next significant someone.

I often say that I don't know why we lost touch for the last couple of years. Technology may have a part in that; it's easier to like, and share, and send a message than it is to meet up. My ex and I were supposed to meet your girlfriend so many times, and things would get cancelled at the last minute, or more likely you'd forget, or lose your phone and not reply to invites in time. My work was shift-based, time was precious. Or maybe we were both just settled in our ways, and that little line of writing was enough. Whatever the reason, I wish I had tried harder to make those meets take place instead of getting irritated and chucking your Earl Grey brew down the sink in annoyance. I wish I had just got in my car, driven to your flat, and posted your favourite specially-made flapjacks through the letterbox. Shown you how much you still sat in my heart.

Even so, in 2018, I was the third person you called after your sister and your girlfriend to share the latest news that this time, it was secondary. This time, it was everywhere. And this time, it was terminal.

And it can't get any worse than that. Nothing has ever felt worse than that. The network that sprang up from that moment, as I realised after each phone call just how many women we were connected to through you, was quite something. And this time, we all had the one thought in common, like a collective consciousness. We were all going to miss you so fucking much. You had been at the centre of all of us coming together and knowing each other. We, at one stage or another, had all fallen under your cool gaze and loved you and each other in so many different ways. My relationship had begun to break down a few months before and by then, it was hanging by a thread. I wanted to give it one more go, and somehow still give you what you deserved from your lifelong fan club.

We all think that you thought you'd beat it. Maybe that's why you didn't follow doctor's orders or stay still for long enough to finalise a meet-up. You told me which hospital you were in but forget to say which ward, then you'd be at home, then at your sister's, then with your girlfriend, but always totally useless at meeting up.

My youngest son was having his birthday party at home. The family was there, and there was an air of chaos as multiple pizza flavours were being compiled. I went up to the bathroom for two minutes of quiet when my air and stuffing suddenly left me. I felt myself turn transparent and back again in an instant. I had to sit on the side of the bath, and I felt every follicle stand on end. And then I felt calm, like someone switched off the extractor fan in the kitchen, and everything was silent.

Later conversations confirmed that my experience had coincided with the time that you left us. Left your legacy within us and a love that feels overflowing and yet hollowed out all at the same time, but life-defining in so many ways. You touched and changed a lot of lives. We, your tribe, aren't as close with each other as we each individually felt we were with you. That's okay. We're okay. It was comforting in some ways to find out that there was more than just myself who didn't get to you in those last few months. Our mutual friend who did see you told me that you just couldn't muster your goodbye for me. I do understand how hard it is to find the words.

Claire and I finally met at your funeral. That's not one, but two great meet-cute stories, both with you at the centre. You'd fucking love that. I think that its helped us both with our grief to find time to share our memories of you, something which we still do regularly. Claire had your beautiful, huge brown eye tattooed on her wrist. I sometimes stare into that image when she's sleeping next to me, and I wonder if you can see me looking at you.

You're Such a Good Pup

Pup Teddy

"YOU'RE SUCH A GOOD pup." Those immortal words are said to a human puppy and usually accompanied by an ear scratch, tummy rub, or head pat. It sends shivers of joy and adulation down my spine. What do I do with the praise now? Nuzzle my handler's leg in appreciation, sit and look content with being good, do something cute, or bring my handler a toy to say thanks for calling me a good pup? The options are endless but no matter what I decide, being called a good pup gives me a warm, fuzzy glow on the inside, because I know I've pleased my handler.

At university, I made some amazing friends within the gay community. After graduating, we went our separate ways but stayed in touch. One friend ended up in London, and the other in Manchester, two cities with their own distinct, out and proud queer community. Up until this point, I would have considered myself sexually open-minded and confident. However, that was put to the test when I started visiting London and Manchester.

Manchester, in particular, has a vibrant and diverse kink, fetish, and alternative scene. On any given weekend, there's a mass of rubber and latex, masters and slaves, bears, scallies, otters, and many more subcultures and communities socialising, eating, drinking, and sometimes getting intimate come the early hours of the morning. The fragrant aroma of poppers, rubber, and sweat fills your nostrils as it emanates from the bars and clubs from early evening until the small hours of the next day. My first ever experience of this was, I'll admit, a little unnerving. A mix of awe, amazement, excitement, and confusion meant I wanted to run away but also stay and experience everything all at once.

I had so many questions. But then, for the first time, I saw one from the corner of my eye—a human wearing what I now know to be called a pup hood. It was a completely new phenomenon to me, so I curiously, and with some apprehension, asked my friend what it was all about. As he explained it to me, my stomach went into nervous knots, akin to the feeling you get just before setting off in the front car of a roller coaster.

"Ownership and submission."

"Social play and sex play."

"A headspace away from reality."

All these comments and phrases amassed in my head, uncontrollably swirling around. Is this me? Could I be a human pup? It certainly sounded intriguing...

***

The years went by with many more visits to Manchester and London. The kink and fetish scenes became my home-from-home, and it's where I felt completely comfortable. It brought that sense of belonging, freedom, and personal discovery. That's no mean feat for a slightly overweight, hairy guy in what can often be a fickle world of stereotypically attractive, smooth, toned guys. My understanding of, and yearning to explore, the world of human puppy play grew like a well-watered sunflower and became ever more intense. When 2019 rolled around, I took the plunge and purchased my first ever pup hood. It was only cheap (from a well-known online retailer), but it was mine. My very own pup hood. Made from neoprene, the ears and muzzle were blue, and the rest was black. I wondered how it would feel putting it on for the first time. Would I just feel stupid? What if it didn't fit?

It fit like a glove. And I didn't feel stupid at all. In fact, it felt *so* right. Having put it on, the most natural thing seemed to be to drop to my paws (that's onto your hands and knees in human speak). My heart was pounding, my stomach in my throat. Why had I waited so long to try this? The world around me stopped in that moment. Nothing else mattered. Without realizing it, I let out a small yelp of a bark, not dissimilar to the famous lion cub from Pride Rock. I had a voice. Granted, I sounded more like a startled kitten than a dog, so it needed work, but I'd finally discovered *me*. I knew exactly what other pups meant when they said puppies often enter a headspace in their hood. Over the next few weeks, I added the clothing and accessories associated with being a pup to my collection. T-shirts, paws for my hands, oversized nose ring for my hood, and matching neoprene top and shorts.

My second "Oh, wow" moment came when I got my name tag. I

bought a chain collar and padlock to attach my new name tag to. In my excitement, I'd decided to go to a high street pet shop to get a bone-shaped name tag. The shop worker was very confused when I asked for Teddy to be printed on both sides. No contact information, no vet information, and no other info–just the name, Teddy. The shop assistant proceeded to tell me in great detail the law around having identifiable information on name tags for pets. I went bright red and became increasingly uneasy. I didn't have the confidence to tell them it was for me, so I smiled nicely and wished they'd just shut up and print my dog tag.

I ran out of the shop and breathed a huge sigh of relief. When I got home, putting on my hood, chain collar, and attaching my name tag made me feel complete. I had a puppy identity and a strange feeling of pride to have my padlock and name tag, showing that, as a pup, I was owned by someone (in my case, my handler). My bark had come on leaps and bounds too. It was somewhere between a terrier yap and a Labrador bark.

Side note: When I first started to physically discover my sexuality, I realised that whether I liked it or not, I was considered a cub or bear. A slightly larger body shape and a hairy chest made this inevitable. That's where my pup name came from. From bear to teddy bear, I got Teddy (or Ted, for short). It encompasses the intersectionality between my queer identities.

***

In the summer of 2019, I went to my first puppy social event as Teddy in Manchester. I was incredibly nervous. The room had around forty other puppies and handlers. There were soft mats on the floor, lots of dog toys (squeaky toys, footballs, tug toys, etc.) and an amazing atmosphere. Feeling completely out of my depth, I promptly propped up the bar and had a couple of strong drinks for a bit of courage. I watched with intrigue in a not too dissimilar way to a young puppy watching its owners, and I took in what was happening. Tug of war with rope toys. Pups sent into a manic spin by squeaky toys. Others just enjoying a tummy rub and cuddle. With sufficient liquid confidence consumed, I went for it. Straight away, puppies I didn't know came over and invited me to be involved. Before I knew it, three hours had gone by, and I was in my element. I underestimated the feeling of being in a different mindset and headspace. I felt free and energized. I wanted to know more and decided then and there that I would definitely be back.

Just when I thought it was over, a puppy asked me if I was coming to the second part of the event. I looked very confused. I thought I did cute puppy dog eyes, but I think I just looked perplexed and possibly like I was in pain. Not put off by this look, the puppy told me the second part was in a bar that I knew well and how it was more about the kink side of pup play, rather than the social side. Intrigued, I took the wristband they were offering and went in.

This was the point in my journey to human pup discovery that I realised I wasn't as sexually well-versed as I thought I was. In fact, it became apparent very quickly that I was a bit of a novice at anything outside of mild to moderate kink, despite many years in and around Manchester and London. The organisers provided everything you could possibly think of: rope, bondage tape, clothes pegs, and my nemesis, pinwheels! As someone who is particularly ticklish, pinwheels are the evilest, yet most unbelievably satisfying, piece of kink kit I've come across. The distinctive smell of poppers and an almost visible layer of musk and testosterone permeated the air. I had another drink and threw myself into the melee of semi-naked human pups, quite literally, headfirst.

It was strangely less about having sex than I'd initially thought it would be. But the liberation it brought, the ability to explore your undiscovered kinks, or to satisfy that urge you've had to try something new, or do that one thing that just gets you off every time was mesmerizing. The feeling of being completely free, often wearing nothing but your pup hood and a jock strap (and sometimes even less than that) and being in a place where everyone had complete mutual respect regardless of body shape, age, race, or disability was just euphoric. Even some of the bar staff were puppies. I'd been to this bar many times before, but I'd never felt like this. The excitement, anticipation, and sexual tension were palpable. Despite not being my human self, I felt more like myself than I had for a long time. The next five hours were revealing, in more ways than one, with a crash course in ropes and bondage tape and the most fun I'd had in a long time, despite being teased constantly with pinwheels. Note to self–never tell another puppy you're ticklish. My puppy kink virginity had well and truly been taken.

You're Such a Good Pup

Over the next nine months, I regularly went to Manchester, London, and Birmingham pup events and each time, I grew with confidence. The world of kink and fetish is often seen by those outside it as creepy, sordid, and dirty. I've found that to be as far from the truth as you can get. The pup community is a small but wonderful one to belong to. Respect, fun, socializing, and yes, sometimes, the most amazing and powerful sex you've ever experienced, are at the heart of what puppy play is all about. The COVID pandemic put the brakes on face-to-face puppy social events, but they still carried on virtually throughout 2020 and 2021. Now into 2022, social events and meet-ups have started again in earnest and are busier and more fun than ever.

So, the next time someone tells you something that's different about themselves—don't judge them. You never know, you might just like it too.

Jen

Tray Morgan

Jen, her name was. Fem Jen.
She had long blond hair that fell
all the way down her pale, pinky-white back.
Chardonnay eyes that sparkled like crystal
cut glass when caught by sunlight.

She was my secret.

Every fibre of my being awoke
in her embrace, her kiss,
with every stroke, skin to skin.

Her lips to mine brought me to life.
She was the air I sorely needed in a
barren life. She was the warmth of
a nurturing sun. The gentle breeze
that soothed me.

No one knew.
Just me and her.
Stealing time together.

My beautiful, exquisite secret.

Soulmate

Saffron Sage

THE FIRST TIME I MET you, I really disliked you. You ruffled my aura, and I found you obnoxious and rude. The second time we met, you cheekily borrowed a cigarette and asked if I wanted to go for a pint.

You became my friend, made me smile, and your warped sense of humour made me laugh. You dragged me to the pub and got me to dance, have fun again, be more carefree, and not care what people thought of me. The dolphin tattoo on your left arm made me go quiet when I first saw it, and you asked what was wrong. How could I explain that you're my divine serendipity when I least expected to find you in my life, and that I left my toxic relationship after seeing a pod of dolphins?

You already thought I was a fruit loop due to my belief in Reiki, my crystals, my alternative beliefs, and alternative therapies. Your touch was electric, and you made me melt with sensuality when you first kissed me, turning my knees to jelly. You made me feel like a real woman again and opened up all my desires. Your eyes can read deep into my soul.

I know I've met you before in a past life. Our connection is deeper than this life alone could create. It's centuries of love, longing, desire, and beauty.

In this life, we left our previous partners to be together and to give our relationship a chance. We chose consciously not to be an affair or a dirty secret. We knew we were worth more than that to each other. I think we were both really brave to make that choice. Knowing we had to give this special connection a chance to grow, despite causing chaos and upsetting friends who didn't agree with our decisions. In our hearts, we knew it was the right thing to do.

I had never been the person who ended a relationship before, and I found it very hard to deal with, even though the relationship had already ended in my eyes. I felt shock and horror when one of my friends called me "the bitch that broke up the relationship." I was tarred as the *other woman.* It created little cuts in my soul, gouged little pieces of me away.

But you healed them. Together, we stood strong.

We persevered through the judgements of others, the hostility, and the blame for our old relationships ending, and we both came out of it stronger. True friends stuck by us, and the others dropped out of our lives. I believe they weren't genuine friends, just acquaintances who had come into our life for a reason and then left. That balance is part of life, part of being, and I've learned to accept it.

You gave me my moonstone to keep me balanced. I never take it off, and I carry a piece of you with me always. Balance doesn't always mean agreement though. We have our differences, things which complement one another.

You like football, and I like rugby. You do things to embarrass me, like touching my bum in the supermarket, and you laugh when I turn red. We are totally Yin and Yang. Cancer and Aries aren't supposed to be destined to last this long in a relationship. We are total opposites, but somehow it works. You are my rock, my confidante, and my best friend. You make me ponder things deeply so that I change and grow.

Once, you asked me, "Who is the real you?" You said that I needed to find myself and find my own way. You described me as a caterpillar nibbling away at a little leaf, existing but not yet living a full life. And then I underwent a metamorphosis and turned into a beautiful, colourful butterfly. I agreed with you, and I like that you see me that way.

You call me your pili pala, Welsh for butterfly, and it's the most endearing term you use. You encouraged me to spread my wings and fly. You dragged me for walks with the dogs, got me lost in the dark, and made life an adventure again. You stand by me through thick and thin and defend my corner. You are my rottweiler and make me feel safe again. You hug me and hold me through the tough hard times.

You were there for me through COVID and were my emotional support even though *you* gave me the bloody virus! Unlike so many other people during the pandemic, lockdown made us closer and stronger. Other couples around us were splitting up and divorcing as they found they didn't like each other quite as much as they thought when they were forced into 24/7 contact.

But I couldn't get enough of you.

I love waking up next to you, and I have no regrets. You are my Aphrodite, my Greek goddess, and so opposite to my Welsh warrior side. You're still my unexpected life blessing, and you were sent into my life for all the right reasons.

I love you with all my heart, body, and soul. You are my soulmate, and you make my life complete. I love you with all my whole, authentic, and quirky lesbian self.

The Conversation

Tray Morgan

I'M HERE AS AN observer with Mrs Bradshaw and eight of the children she teaches in secondary school, all approximately fourteen years old. Mrs Bradshaw, who I'll refer to from now on as Mrs B, is trialling some small group conversations to aid the school in meeting their legal requirements to provide relationship education. Today's short conversation is on the topic of LGBT.

"But you have to identify yourself somehow." Marshall is a young-looking lad, with mousy short hair who seems to think that everyone should identify as something.

"No, I don't," says Emily. Her voice is strikingly clear and calm and cuts across the air from the opposite side of the table.

Clearly a difference of opinion is in motion as they stare at each other. I find myself agreeing with Emily. Why should she label herself if she doesn't want to?

"Oh, Miss!" exclaims Tiffany. Her head juts out from behind Emily, whom she is sat beside as she attempts to gain Mrs B's attention. "There are so many labels," says Tiffany. "It's very confusing." Tiffany has red curly locks, a dimpled face, and makes a very good point.

I'm fifty-three, and I find the array of labels one has to choose from now quite dizzying. A number of them I've never even heard of.

"Mrs Bradshaw," says Adam, seated beside Marshall. "Why do we have to talk about LGBT stuff today?"

I notice Clive, seated next to Adam, sit up sharply, appearing swiftly animated. "She has to," he says. "All secondary schools are required to provide Relationship Education and Sexual Orientation at comprehensive schools like this one."

No, they didn't do this when I was at school. It is, in a way, somehow healing to be here with children talking on this subject and so far, it has been a pleasant experience.

"We spoke about types of *sexual* relationships in the other group," says Selina. "This group is to talk about LGBT *families*."

I see Adam smile, but it's Clive who speaks.

"LGBT people do have sex, you know," says Clive.

"I know," says Selina. "I was at that class too! But this isn't just about sex."

Adam and Clive giggle together whilst everyone else either smiles or stifles a laugh.

It strikes me they are so young and yet capable of such an adult conversation, in their own way. The only dialogue I heard at school on this subject were taunts with aggression and hostility. It wasn't safe to be gay or even thought to be gay.

"So, children," says Mrs B. "We all know why we're here. Firstly, so I can see how much awareness you currently have, who can tell me what LGBT refers to?"

"Gay people," says Adam, although Emily is the one with her hand up.

"LGBT is an acronym," says Mrs B.

I curse the overuse in our society of the acronym. I'm dyslexic and get words, let alone letters, the wrong way around from time to time. Which is fine as long as the people you're speaking with aren't touchy-sensitive or emotionally volatile when you get something wrong.

"So," says Mrs B, "anyone know what LGBT stands for?"

Emily still has her hand up.

"Emily," says Mrs B.

"Acronyms are usually formed from the initial letters of words," says Emily.

"Yes. So what do you think LGBT stands for?" asks Mrs B.

"Lesbian, Gay, Bisexual, Transgender," says Emily.

Selina, sitting beside Emily, nods enthusiastically to show her agreement.

"Mrs Bradshaw," says Clive. "Most places have a plus sign at the end of LGBT."

"And what does the plus sign signify?" asks Mrs B.

"That there are other identities," says Tiff.

This conversation takes my breath away. I'd never heard of transgender, for example, until I left school. The children here are so aware of the society they live in that a wave of relief filters over me. Perhaps there is hope for our society yet.

"Very good," says Mrs B. "And the type of families LGBT people create? What do you know about that? Tiffany," asks Mrs B, on seeing Tiffany raise her hand.

"Tiff, please," says Tiffany. "LGBT people adopt their children, don't they?"

"Some do," says Mrs B. "How else could LGBT people form a family?"

"Jessica, in pottery," says Selina loudly, "she has two mummies and one of her mummies has a boyfriend."

"Is she bisexual then?" asks Dylan, appearing suddenly interested in the conversation as he turns in his seat to face her more squarely.

"I don't know," says Selina, sounding indignant. "I didn't ask."

A part of me is pleased to hear Selina didn't ask. Boundaries at age fourteen is quite an achievement. Assuming that's why she didn't ask, of course.

"What else, children?" asks Mrs B.

The young people fell silent. The ticking clock seems to denote they're thinking the question over. At their age, I didn't have a clue.

"By being together," says Emily, "in their relationship. People don't have to have children to be a family. My Aunt Grace and Uncle James don't have children, and they're family to each other."

"I agree," says Mrs B. "So, you all have quite a bit of knowledge between you, that's good. I like that you're sharing what you know with each other. So, when it comes to identity, you were speaking about that a little while ago. Marshall, I believe I heard you say that people *needed* to identify themselves in some way."

"Yes, Mrs Bradshaw," says Marshall. "How else can anyone, including them, know who or what they are if a person doesn't identify in some recognisable way?"

"Well, let's discuss that, shall we?" asks Mrs B.

I like the way she poses it as a question and statement at the same time.

"Emily, I believe you had a different opinion," says Mrs B.

Emily shrugs. "I'm a HB," she says.

"Do you mean human being, Emily?" asks Mrs B.

Emily nods. "Yes, Mrs Bradshaw, I do."

"I feel the same as Emily," says Tiff.

"Me too," says Selina, who sits bolt upright, her head up and her eyes alight. "I'm annoyed," she says. "Emily is right."

There is quiet in the class as if everyone expects Selina to say more but she doesn't.

"Can you elaborate?" asks Mrs B.

"Um... elab-o-r-ate," says Selina. She appears uncertain as to what she is meant to do.

Dylan gives Selina a playful nudge with his elbow. "What's Emily right about?" he asks.

"If Emily doesn't want to label herself other than her name and that she's human, then Emily ought to be able to do that," says Selina.

"Yeah, we're meant to be equal to each other," says Clive.

Mrs B smiles at hearing this comment. "And what does it mean to be equal to one another?" she asks.

"Ooh, I know, Mrs Bradshaw," says Adam, as he shoots his hand up into the air.

"Go ahead, Adam," says Mrs B.

"Treated fairly, equally, with equal rights," says Adam.

"Well done," says Mrs B. "Anything else?"

Really? More? What's been said didn't enter my mind until much later in my life.

"Having equal chances and options," says Tiff.

"Not being discriminated against," says Marshall.

"What do you know about the discrimination that LGBT people face?" asks Mrs B.

All eight young people sit quietly. I notice Marshall and Clive look as if they want to speak but both appear uncertain if they should, or perhaps they don't know how? Little Lucy, sitting between Clive and Dylan, hasn't spoken a word yet. I wonder if she will. I'm rooting for her to. Perhaps I see a part of myself in her. The quiet girl in the class who never found her voice. I hope Lucy finds hers.

"Think about what was said a little while ago about equality," says Mrs B.

Tiffany's hand shoots into the air. "My sister didn't get a job once," says Tiff. "She said she was discriminated against."

"Did she say how?" asks Mrs B.

"Well, she said the interview had gone really well," says Tiff. "It was towards the end, when they were talking about the perks of working at this company, some of it extended to spouses, so my sister asked if her partner, Hilary, would receive them too as they aren't married but do live with each other, and my sister said the temperature in the room changed," says Tiff. "She said there was a serious temperature drop."

Now this I can believe, even though it's now meant to be illegal. But how are you supposed to prove it?

"Well," says Adam, "if they don't want LGBT people in their company, shouldn't they be allowed to decide that? It's their company."

"Well, think that through," says Mrs B. "If people were allowed to not employ suitably qualified candidates because they don't personally like them, what difficulties do you think that might cause?"

Silence fills the room. One by one, each teenager turns to look at Adam. I find my gaze joining theirs.

"I don't know," says Adam.

"I don't like garden peas, but my daddies say I still have to eat them," says Lucy. "They say they're good for me."

I can see her line of thinking and wonder if she'll follow it through to its conclusion.

Adam frowned. "Are you saying LGBT people are good for me?" he asks.

"My dads are good for me," says Lucy. Her eyes light up when she says this. Her voice is loud for such a small girl who, until now, had not spoken a word.

"You have two dads?" asks Adam.

"Yes, I do," says Lucy. "The issue isn't having different types of families, it's that people automatically assume that everyone has one dad and one mum. I have two dads. I love them, and they love me."

"Adam," says Emily and fixes her gaze on him. "Who gets to decide who is likeable and who isn't?"

"Yeah," says Dylan. "Why shouldn't my uncle have a job just because someone who already works at a company doesn't like him or something about him?"

Adam shrugs. "I'd not thought of it like that," he says. "I guess it's like when I wanted to join in the game of football that time, but Brian wouldn't let me."

"Exactly," says Dylan.

"If someone is LGBT or not, that shouldn't matter," says Clive.

"Why not?" asks Mrs B.

"LGBT people are just people," says Clive. "They're just like anyone else, really."

My heart melts. LGBT people are just *people*. How beautiful that they recognize this.

"I've never met anyone who is LGBT," says Adam.

"Yes, you have," says Dylan. "I told you I like boys *and* girls, remember?"

"Oh, yeah," says Adam and appears momentarily embarrassed. "I forgot." He grins. "Correction, I do know someone."

"So, are you bisexual then, Dylan?" asks Emily.

"That's a term that speaks to me," says Dylan.

I admit, I'm amazed. Age fourteen, and Dylan not only knows his sexuality but appears to be perfectly comfortable with it. Things have progressed in our schools. I wish my school experience had been like this.

"Now, children," says Mrs B. "You all know that sexuality is on a continuum."

"Ooh, like that programme my dad liked?" asks Clive. "There were people from the future who came back to our present to change things in their own time, our future. The characters created another timeline so there's two of everyone." Clive pauses, appearing not to know whether he should or shouldn't feel excited about what he was about to say. "Do you think it's possible that I have a different sexuality in a different timeline from now?" he asks.

"Well," says Mrs B, "that wasn't what I had in mind." She looks thoughtful and then continues, "I'm in no position to tell you if there are alternative timelines or whether your sexuality will change or not over time."

"My uncle is gay," says Dylan.

I notice what appears to be a shadow of some kind fall across Dylan's face. I've seen similar shadows before.

"He was hurt the other day when he left a pub in town," says Dylan.

"Was that because he's gay?" asks Tiff.

Dylan nods, his frown deepening.

"It's not fair to be hurt by people for any reason, but especially for being what you are," says Selina.

"It's not fair to be beaten up," whispers Lucy. "One of my daddies was once."

"I'm sorry to hear that," says Mrs B. "And you, Dylan, for your uncle. You're quite right, it isn't fair at all. Are your daddies okay, Lucy?"

"Oh, yes," says Lucy, smiling. "They're lovely."

Mrs B smiles a gentle smile. "Dylan, is your uncle okay?"

"Yes," says Dylan. That cheeky smile from earlier reappears on Dylan's face. "He's lovely too."

"Good," says Mrs B, ignoring Marshall and Adam's snorts of stifled laughter. "Children, hear me, please."

The young people fall into silence, their collective group gaze on Mrs B.

"We all have a right to our thoughts and feelings," says Mrs B, "but none of us has a right to express our thoughts and feelings in whatever way we like, without considering the hurt that might be caused by our doing so. There must be consequences."

"Consequences?" asks Clive.

"Yeah," says Dylan. "Like when you pushed me down the hill, and I got up and pushed you back."

"I was thinking more along the lines of non-violent actions," says Mrs B.

They all sit still and are silent.

For a moment, I wonder what will happen next. Then I notice the young people are glancing at each other, and they all turn to look at Mrs B and say in unison, "Yes, Mrs Bradshaw."

There is an air of regard for Mrs B from these teenagers.

"Why do you think there are LGBT events?" asks Mrs B. "Or conversations specifically organised like the one we're having today?"

"Ooh, I know," says Tiff. "To break down prejudice."

"And what is prejudice?" asks Mrs B.

"When you dislike someone," says Dylan, "and think it's okay to hurt them for it, which it isn't."

"Are there certain things that come to mind?" asks Mrs B.

"Because of skin colour or religion," says Marshall. "Or because they're gay."

"That's not the only excuses some people use," says Dylan.

"No," says Emily. "They're some of the ones in the law that are not allowed though."

"And what else? Why LGBT events specifically, anything?" asks Mrs B.

"So people can see LGBT people for who they are," says Selina. "Like Clive said, just people."

The room falls quiet as if everyone is contemplating what's been said. What I would have given at their age to have just one friend who thought this way.

"While that's true," say Clive, "I understand Emily's view of not wanting to label herself too. Like, when you label yourself, people can see you as that thing permanently, but you might change. If you're just human, then you can be anything you want."

"Everyone has their own way of looking at things, don't they?" says Tiff.

"That's right," says Mrs B. "It's important for all of us to remember that for as many people as there are, there are that many worlds too."

"Ooh, Clive, your parallel universe theory," says Marshall. "You really could be on to something."

Laughter flutters around the room

"Well, children, thank you," says Mrs B. "I appreciate our open dialogue. I wish the rest of the world was more like you."

"In what way?" asks Emily, appearing curious.

"You've all shared your feelings and thoughts on what is still a sensitive subject in our society," says Mrs B. "Even with the improvements made over the years. Once upon a time, it wasn't safe to be seen holding hands with one's partner in public and in some places, it still isn't."

The young people sit quietly as if mulling over what Mrs B has said. I envy her and the children. To have a dialogue as they are today would have been everything to me at their age, and here with them now, I can see this is just another day at school for them.

"You've all spoken and listened to each other," continues Mrs B, "and where you've disagreed, you've accepted the other's point of view, not attacked it."

This in itself is a major achievement, given the way a lot of adults behave.

"You've been curious to know more," Mrs B goes on, "and you want to understand. I hope you all hold on to these qualities. Treat other people with kindness and dignity and keep trying to understand each other."

"Mrs Bradshaw," says Clive. "When you said about not being able to hold hands with your partner?" He pauses, as if he is considering whether to say what he is thinking. "Were you speaking about you?"

All the young people look expectantly at Mrs B.

"That's very perceptive of you," says Mrs B. "I was, yes."

"So are you a lesbian or bisexual?" asks Tiff.

"I prefer gay woman, if you don't mind," says Mrs B.

"Not at all," says Tiff.

There is a moment's quiet as if the whole class are absorbing the news. My heart bursts to know there's an openly gay teacher in this school. That never happened in my day. There were gay teachers, obviously, but no one knew about it. I remember some teachers lost their jobs, and some even had to move away from the area when people found out. But then, people used to believe being gay meant you were unsafe for children, which isn't true.

"Mrs Bradshaw," says Lucy.

"Yes?"

"You're such a nice person," says Lucy. "You really do care about all of us, don't you?"

"I do."

They all look thoughtful, but it's Clive who speaks again.

"Mrs Bradshaw," says Clive. "I think I'd like to be a les...I mean, gay lady, like you when I grow up," he says.

A Life in the Wrong Body
Sam Stormborn

As a toddler I would say, "Before I was a girl, when I was a boy..."
Growing up, I would hope and pray my body might change and bring me joy.

Each day my mother dressed me for school, but I always had a deceitful plan,
I'd be dressed in a skirt as a rule but hidden in my bag were the clothes of a young man.

Having older brothers is kind of a blessing, hand-me-down clothes was kind of cool,
Whilst I hated the way I was dressing; I'd turn to a boy when I got to school.

I watched my peers through their puberty, with bumps growing in all the right places,
It wasn't going to happen to me, I had heard of other individual cases.

Maybe I would be the lucky one, maybe for me life would be a breeze,
I wouldn't be like just anyone, my development would cease.

As the years rolled by it was looking positive, thirteen years of age went by without changing,
Another year went by, my hormones dispositive, I felt good, stood tall, my heart would sing.

"You, boy!" I would hear at school, and my face would turn to a smile,
To hear it sounded really cool, and I'd hold that feeling for a while.

"Can I help you, sir?" I would hear in shops. "Thank you," I would reply

with a mighty grin,
That feeling? I hope it never stops, but still, these secrets I kept from my kin.

I turned fifteen in 1983. I was still living a life without surrender,
At home I was referred to as she, elsewhere people were unsure of my gender.

You have to understand back then it was hard, LGBTQ+ as a subject taboo,
Transgender as a discussion was wholly barred, children weren't allowed a point of view.

Three months before turning sixteen, it started just like any other day,
Before Mother Nature shattered my dreams, my image in the mirror turned pale and grey.

My life as I knew it had come to an end, my life as I knew it would be no more,
This time I wanted my life to end, my gender couldn't be changed by the clothes I wore.

From this point forward I lived a lie, pretending to be someone I'm not,
Just existing, watching each day go by, waiting for the day in a grave I would rot.

At the age of fifty I finally came out, a heavy weight lifted from my mind,
From the rooftops I wanted to shout, but complications left a bind.

My choices are no longer about me, my options dictated by circumstance and time,
I long for the day I will finally be free, to live a life that is finally mine.

Your Truest Nature

Vanessa Ball

Part 1: The Wilderness Lives within You

The wilderness lives within you.
Your nature is wild and free
Ever changing with the seasons.

Dance beneath the morning sun,
Sway and bend under
The starry night sky.

Breath and pulse.
Rise and fall.
Love and live
Until your time is called.

Pure and gentle.
You bring wonder to the eye.
Nature at work.
Harmony in play.

Simple yet perfect.
Silent and beautiful.

The wilderness lives within you.

Part 2: How Do You Love?

I am open to all.
I can love
Whoever comes to me

Vanessa Ball

With a pure heart
Full of the right intention.

Who can love me?
All of me.

Someone who doesn't
Wish to control
Suppress or own me.
But who wants to see me flourish
Like the wild flower I am.

Because
The wilderness lives within me
And I embody
All its power and allure.

My Father's Son

AP Bramley

FAMILY GATHERINGS ARE ALWAYS interesting. A delight for some and an ordeal for others. And for lucky old me, a chance to be both. I used to love seeing my family, used to count down the days until my grandad's next ridiculous garden party filled with balloons and games for the kids. I used to love chattering, or debating, with my grandad and uncles about literally anything and everything under the sun. But as time went on and I flew further and further away from the conglomeration of nests all down the road from each other, those gatherings happened less and less. It took a wedding for me to see them all again.

"Congratulations!" I said to the lucky couple as soon as I heard the news. My husband and I were at my dad's house for a visit when they came round, and out of everything, it was the most recent and happiest news to focus on.

The bride to be, Lou, smiled at us with only a hint of tiredness. "Thank you. Took us long enough, didn't it?"

"How long have you been together?" my husband asked.

"Twenty-seven years," my grandad said, already slumped into the nearest chair. "She finally wore me down enough to say yes."

Lou scowled at him while the rest of us chuckled.

"Is that why you're only giving yourself a month to put a wedding together? Less time for him to get cold feet?" Dad asked from the kitchen as he fetched drinks in between fending off two children desperate for sweets.

"Oh, that," Lou said. "We need to wait a minimum of twenty-eight days, and that was the soonest date they had. Well, there was that one and one at eleven-ish, but that's much too early I think."

Grandad grunted in agreement. I grabbed my drink and my husband's and went to sit down. "I'm honestly surprised you're having a whole ceremony and reception. I thought you two would just elope. Like, one day we'd get a call, and you two had got married in Scarborough or something."

"I wanted to! She wouldn't let me."

And so the conversation went on, discussing the plan so far: which registry office it was going to be, the hall hired out for the reception, all the basics, really.

"So," Lou turned to me and smiled, "I know you're all grown up and married now, but we were hoping to have all the grandkids for the bridal party, if you were happy to do that?"

I smiled through the vice tightening around my chest. "Sure, I'd love to." I tried to be happy for them and ignore the growing dread that was kicking my heart rate into overdrive. "Does that mean...dresses?"

"Well, that's up to you," Lou said. "My granddaughter, Dana, has already said that she doesn't want to wear a dress. Which I don't blame her. I'm tempted to wear a suit myself. It's much more comfortable than a dress."

"If we eloped, you could show up in your jeans," Grandad called out from the other side of the room.

He grinned, Lou scowled, and they both seemed to miss the growing tension in my shoulders. I looked to my dad, to his partner, to my husband. Everyone else here knew. They would help me if I asked. And this would be the best time to tell Grandad and Lou some news of my own. There was no reason for me to be so scared, but I had to clasp my hands together to stop them shaking as I turned to Lou with my best attempt at a casual smile. "I think I would prefer a suit as well." I took a breath, the next words on my tongue.

"That's fine," Lou said. "If you send me over your sizes, I'll get something picked out for you to try on."

And the moment was gone. The secret froze in my mouth, and all I could do was smile and lean back into my husband, praying that he would ground me.

The conversation moved away from the wedding to other important matters, like Grandad's infernal neighbours and the latest drama with the rest of the family. I joined in with banter of my own, trying to find that energy I used to have around these people with such little effort, while also trying to find the right moment to turn the conversation. The whole time, Sarah, my dad's partner, was glaring at me in a way that asked, "Are you going to tell them?" And when I ignored her look, she obviously decided to *help*.

Grandad and Lou were getting ready to leave. He was getting too tired for company and needed to rest, something he accepted with all the grace of a bull that had just spotted a matador.

"Alex, don't you have something else to tell them before they go?" Sarah said.

And there was the spotlight. Every set of eyes in the room were on me. Perfect. I took a breath that didn't sit right in my lungs and looked at Grandad first. "So...I'm...I'm transgender. Which means that I identify more with...with being a boy? I guess. And I'm asking people to use male terms for me, so he and him, husband, son, grandson. That kind of thing–if that's okay."

Before anyone responded, my mind was filled with the most horrific ways this could play out. Him snorting in disbelief or screwing up his face in disgust. There was no reason for me to think that; he'd never done anything like that to me before. But after everyone else who I'd come out to had reacted so well, I was terrified of this being the one that would break the trend. And it couldn't be my grandad who became the coming out story that went wrong. It couldn't.

I blinked.

And Grandad just shrugged and said, "Okay."

Lou smiled. "Don't worry. Dana has a girlfriend. You're not our first LGBT grandkid."

And just like that it was done. And everyone was fine. Everyone now knew the truth, knew my new identity. Everyone was fine. The weight that came off my chest left me trembling in relief and in desperate need of a strong drink. I'd be going to their wedding and be part of their bridal party in a suit, alongside my apparently sapphic cousin. And just like that, all my worries about the wedding were eased.

Until the suits were being ordered.

Don't forget to send me your suit sizes. The text came one day. Thankfully, I'd got my first men's suit not a week before, so I had an idea of my measurements. So over they went, without a single concern on my end.

Actually, I'm getting women's suits. I found a lovely ivory one, and I was going to pair them with trainers. Is that okay?

The tennis match of texts that went back and forth was painful to go through. There was no malice, no obvious frustration from her end. But that didn't stop me from panicking while picturing a small ivory jacket that tucked in at the waist to show off a lady's wonderful natural curves, paired with slim cut trousers flaring over the hips before clinging to thin, elegant legs. My skin burned with the thought of wearing something like that.

My husband, wonderful man that he is, couldn't quite understand why I was freaking out so much over clothes. Because they *are* just clothes. I know that they're just clothes. Rationally, there was no reason to panic over such a small thing. And I could put up with them for one day. Not even a full day, in fact. The wedding was mid-afternoon and would go straight into an evening reception. I would be in the outfit for what, eight hours if we stayed for the full reception? That was a day at work, and I would be able to drink for most of it.

But it wasn't that simple. I couldn't explain to him why the thought of this hypothetically incredibly feminine suit filled me with such dread. I couldn't even explain all the reasons to myself. All I knew was everything in me wanted to reject the idea. But how easy is that to do when it's someone else's special day? When they're already accommodating our needs to some degree? And when they have so many other things to plan, and they're buying me the damn thing. I gave Lou my measurements as well as I could, seeing as I hadn't bought women's clothes in at least a year, and asked for pictures of the suit so I knew what I was in for.

A square cut jacket and slouch style trousers, paired with white floral Vans. Nothing about it would be accenting curves I'd want to hide, and there were no heels or sequins. It wasn't what I would have picked for myself, but it definitely wasn't the worst. As long as the fit worked as designed, then most of my dysphoria should be sated. When they came around to let me try it on, the suit jacket was actually a size or two too big, not to the point of swamping me though. And if it helped hide my hips, I wasn't going to complain. This was when I warned my grandparents that I did, in fact, wear a chest binder so any shirt collar lower than your typical V-neck would show it off to all the guests. Grandad shrugged and said it didn't matter, while Lou described the blouse and worried over not bringing it over for me to try on. I even showed them the binder—not the full thing as I didn't fancy showing off my underwear to my grandparents—just the collar, so they could see how high it sits. The blouse would definitely show it off. But they assured me that it was fine, and they left to prepare the rest of the wedding.

The second the door closed and my husband said, "Well, that wasn't so bad," everything came out. The suit was still wrong. It fit fine, there was no physical dysphoria in the thing, but it still felt wrong. And I hadn't worked it out until Grandad had described what he would be wearing. Along with my dad, and Lou's son, and my little brother. All of them would be in grey suits with sage green ties to match the blouses Dana and I were going to wear. Somewhere between coming out to them and the start of the text messages, I realised that I had assumed that Dana and I would be put in the same suit as the groom's party, in the same suit as the men. But no, I was going to be in ivory and trainers along with the "other" adult granddaughter. Yes, I had only just come out to them, and they'd probably been planning all of this before I told them I was trans. And they'd known me my entire life. Of course it was going to take time to adjust, to think of me as a grandson rather than a granddaughter. But that didn't mean it didn't hurt that they grouped me in with the women rather than the men. Because if they had taken the ten seconds to ask me if I wanted a women's or men's suit, I would have leapt at the chance to match my dad and grandad. You could have used me to light up the disco ball at the reception, I would've been that bright, and comfortable, and *happy*.

I understand why they didn't ask. I understand the logic and the reasoning that got us to that point. And my grandparents had other things on their mind. A wedding isn't an easy thing to plan after all. But that didn't mean that it stung any less.

The day of the wedding came around quickly. My husband went out to make sure he had his own outfit, and while doing some last-minute shopping, we found a tie that would match the colour scheme. I promised to tie it for him. We were ready. It was going to be a great day. My worries could park their arses for one bloody day so that I could be there for my grandparents. We even got there early to relieve my worries and make sure I couldn't be the source of any stress.

I had a plan. You see, while I'm not quiet about the fact that I wear a chest binder and I do try to flatten the "girls" (a term used by literally everyone else when they talk about my breasts), I'm about as comfortable showing off said binder as I would be showing off a bra. Which is to say, not at all. No one needs to see my underwear. So, my overnight bag had a backup plan. I would try on the blouse with my binder and with a bra that I hadn't yet got rid of. I would see which one looked better. And I would see if it was more comfortable to have my breasts on display or to have my binder showing.

The first clue that there was a spanner in the works was when I saw the blouse. Lou had picked a loose-fitting shirt, something that she thought both me and her granddaughter would be comfortable in, seeing as neither of us liked feminine styles. And this was definitely loose. Maybe a little too loose. My suspicions were confirmed when I saw the tag and read the shirt size. Once it was on, the shirt looked ready to swallow me and the cuffed sleeves that were meant to come to my elbows went halfway down my forearm. It went past the point of fashionably oversized and into ill-fitting so fast I had to hold back a laugh. This was a fuck-up, I shouldn't laugh. But I couldn't wear a shirt two sizes too big for me.

When Lou saw me in the shirt, her face fell, but I ushered her away. "I can fix it," I told her. "Dad's coming soon to drop off Taylor, I can get him to pick something up. You go get your hair and makeup done."

She was worrying, I could see it, and I had to almost frogmarch her to her beauty stylist while I called my dad. He got my sizes and ran down to the nearest clothes shop. Before long, I had two white men's shirts, one long-sleeved and one short-sleeved, and time to iron out all the creases. My husband even let me steal his brand-new sage green tie so I would still vaguely match the others.

By the time Lou was ready to get dressed, I was in a crisp, white shirt, the ivory suit and trainers, and a sage green tie showing off the Windsor knot I'd managed to learn. And I was beaming. No, I didn't get to wear the same suit as the other men. But I felt like me.

And that was honestly better than I was expecting.

Now came the hard part. Seeing the extended family would be another source of anxiety. The kids were having fun comparing me and my cousin, saying that with our matching suits, glasses, and hair, we looked like twins. Which was cute, and considering how much mine and my cousin's interests had lined up despite a decade apart, it was genuinely nice to hear. But now came the rest. It had been years since I had seen most of them. Forget COVID, the last time most of my grandad's family had seen me was at *my* wedding, when I was the picture of a beautiful bride, gown included.

But it was fine. Because as well as my short hair, subtle undercut, and my trusty binder, I had a pin about the size of a two-pound coin that very conveniently declared to everyone that my pronouns are he and him. Which was a shorthand way of screaming, "Hello! Just to let you know that the little girl that you first met as a snot-nosed rugrat is one of those transgender types you're hearing about on the news. Have fun with that!"

I was *not* going to panic.

Said pin went on my shirt pocket, partly because the buttonhole I would have worn it on was taken up by a beautiful white rose, and partly because I worried that my small badge would be too obnoxious for the wedding photos. Besides, once the ceremony and the pictures were done, the blazer would come off anyway. This way, it was there for when I'd need it, during the one-to-one conversations that were bound to happen before it was deemed socially acceptable to start dancing.

We got to the registry office in a beautiful wedding car. The top was down to let in the wonderful sun. Thankfully, Lou's hair was held together with enough hairspray that an earthquake would struggle to shake it. My cousin and I weren't so lucky.

The kids screeching in front of us were a perfect distraction. When we arrived, Lou had to go for her pre-wedding interview so the rest of us sat in the cool and quiet reception, discussing how we might go down the aisle. The officiant confirmed the little ones, then the big ones, then the bride with her son giving her away.

Wonderful. Beautiful. Nice and simple.

And in the moment before the doors opened, to wave away the last of my nerves, I couldn't help but offer my arm to my cousin with a little bow for comedic effect. We walked slowly, and I smiled at all the family and friends that had gathered. All my feelings went into a little box, shoved way down, because when I saw my grandad and dad standing at the other end of the aisle, there was nothing else I could do. This moment wasn't about me and my perfectly acceptable wedding outfit. It was about them. Twenty-seven years, through thick and thin, and now they were *finally* tying the knot.

When Lou walked down the aisle, Grandad beamed. He and Dad were already holding back the tears, and Dad began to grumble over forgetting his tissues. I held it together until they got to the vows. But when Lou's voice began to tremble over her promise to love and care for her husband, to be there through every sickness, I broke. We all did. The unspoken truth settled on all of us when Lou choked back her tears: in sickness and in health. And Grandad could only look at her with love and gratitude for all her vows and promises. It was beautiful. And despite the bitter edge, it was happy for as long as it could be between them.

The focus on was on the bride and groom after they said, "I do," during the throwing of the confetti, and for all the jokes and banter that came after. The focus stayed on them when everyone moved to the hired hall for the reception, where practically everyone insisted on buying them their first drinks and where people stopped to admire the photo board set up showing their near three decades together. Hugs and congratulations were traded again and again until finally everyone found their seats for the dinner. Grandad had prepared a speech. A very typical grandad speech, it has to be said. One which celebrated not only him and his wife, but the people who had been there for the various bride's and groom's parties.

When he pointed to me, I barely had time to brace myself. "First, is my wonderful granddaughter."

My husband's hand went to my knee to give me a reassuring squeeze as my grandad, loud and proud, declared all my achievements to the hall of his family and friends. I kept on smiling even when his look turned cheeky and he said, "But I still remember her, when she was only up to my knee." He recounted his funniest story of a toddler on holiday at the beach. And I managed to not even shed a single tear. I smiled, hiding my face in my husband's shoulder, trying to focus on his silent, comforting presence. Every wince as Grandad used the wrong pronouns turned into an embarrassed cringe away from ridiculous stories and proud achievements. He moved on, down the line of grandchildren from oldest to youngest, and I kept up my smile and leaned on my husband's shoulder and tried to ignore my aching heart. To the rest of the room I looked like a proud but embarrassed granddaughter. There would be time to correct people later. It was still new. It would take time for people to adjust.

Now I was *very* glad that I had remembered my pronoun badge. And I was antsy to the point that I avoided people I would normally happily catch up with, just in case. I was more than happy to answer any questions, in theory. But I wasn't in the mood for any potential judgement. I had some conversations, all small talk about work, and hobbies, and gossip about people I didn't know about. Finally, one of the uncles spotted my badge and frowned.

It was the first test. I was going into this conversation blind with someone I actually knew really well but whose reaction I couldn't predict. So, I decided to ease into it. "It's my pronoun badge."

"What's one of those?"

Okay, that was to be expected. I smiled and said, "I'm transgender."

"What's that mean?" he asked.

Right. From the beginning it was. He laughed as I sat down, and he joked about how someone sitting down like that was never good. And now I needed to work out how to explain to a man older than my dad what transgender meant. I took it to basics, as oversimplified as they are.

"I don't identify with being female. I more closely identify with being a man, so I would prefer to use he and him pronouns. So, I would be called son, grandson, husband, that kind of thing."

There was no disgust, which was a positive start. There was, however, a lot of confusion. I could see the gears turning. It probably would have made just as much sense to him if I had said all of this in Spanish.

"Oh," he said, light bulb going off, "it's like those men that are wanting to be women to compete in sports."

Oh, shit. My coming out speech wasn't the time to get into the harmful rhetoric currently surrounding that hot button topic, but I couldn't just agree with him. And I couldn't let that impression be the one my uncle was left with about transgender people, like the only reason for someone to transition was for sports.

"Actually," I tried to stay calm as I could feel my defensiveness increase with every moment, "transgender women, so men who become women, actually have to go through rigorous testing before they're allowed to compete. They need to have medically transitioned so that their testosterone is below a certain level and their oestrogen is above a certain level before they can play in any professional sports. And what that does is actually change them physiologically so that their muscle mass changes. Transgender women lose strength when they go on oestrogen."

"Oh, well," he said, "their bones are still stronger, you know."

And this was the moment where I have to admit that I panicked. Up until then, I had never considered that men's bones could be stronger than women's. Different shapes, absolutely. Men are typically taller, have broader shoulders, and narrower hips. More square jawlines. But the idea of bones being stronger was something I had never considered or even heard of. But in that moment, I felt like I couldn't admit that. I couldn't give any quarter to a thought or opinion that led to transphobic thinking. So, I panicked. I doubled down. And I may have added in a little bit of bullshit on my way back to the truth.

"I think you're underestimating how much hormones can do. Granted, they can't change the size and shape of bones. If I ever go on testosterone, I'll never grow any taller. But hormones can change all sort of things physiologically. Bone density, muscle mass, and fat distribution. It's quite incredible really."

Two of those things I knew at the time to be true: testosterone does change muscle mass and where any fat sits on your body, along with all sorts of other wonderful things like lowering your voice, making you grow (and lose) hair. One manic Google search on bones and testosterone after the wedding didn't give an easy consensus one way or the other. As with most medical knowledge around transgender people, more study is needed. And I definitely shouldn't make that claim with such confidence next time.

Thankfully, we were interrupted by my husband before I could dig a deeper hole for myself. And my uncle, with the gears still turning and the confusion still overriding everything else, began to talk about how okay it was. Gay people weren't a thing in his day, and now they're everywhere because they don't need to hide anymore. And it's all great, but people of his generation? It's all new and confusing to him. To which I smiled and fell back into my old patterns. *It's fine. It's a learning process for everyone. People will make mistakes but as long as people try and make an effort then that's all I can ask for.* And with that, my drink was conveniently empty, and I needed to get a new one.

I ended up hiding in the bar for longer than I needed to, just to collect myself. This wasn't the first time I'd been reminded of how much I would have to work to educate other people about this one part of my existence every day. It wasn't the first time I'd been faced with someone who didn't understand, who couldn't wrap their head around it. And it wasn't the first time I had made excuses for them, explained that I understood, that I don't expect the world to be perfect overnight. All in the hopes that the truth pill labelled "This isn't an optional thing" might be a little bit more palatable. Because it isn't optional. You can't just say you accept it and then act exactly the same. You need to try, you need to put in the effort. You need to do the bare minimum to prove that you respect me and my identity enough to change your language and your thinking, and to learn. I don't expect or demand people to know everything about transgender identities overnight. But I want people to prove that they respect me enough, that they care about me enough, to try.

Not one other person asked about the badge. Plenty of people saw it, and I waited for them to ask. But I didn't fancy having that conversation again quite so soon. All I needed was for my patience to wear down or my nerves to be utterly shot before I said the wrong thing to the wrong person, which could've been anyone at that point, and then the mood would be ruined. I didn't want to hurt my grandparents like that. So instead, my husband and I danced quite badly to the cheesy 80s music blasting through the speakers, first with Lou and Dana, then with the kids, then with other aunts. I even snuck in a dance with Dad and Sarah. But most of the time, it was just the two of us. His hand was on my back as we spun around enough to make ourselves dizzy and sang along to all the hits. The nerves melted away with every twirl, shaking off in time with the music. Just like the good old days, when I was in the centre of the dance floor for every disco without fail. The tie and suit jacket were long gone, and the two of us were down to shirt and trousers. And I danced with the man I love, the man who loves every little piece of me, the old and the new, no matter the pronouns I use or the shape I might take one day. And I didn't want to be anywhere else.

When I wasn't dancing, Dana and I were catching up on everything with her dad. She showed me the gigs she'd been to, when she met her favourite actor at a con, and her dog. I told her about the TV shows we'd been watching, gave her advice on the tattoos she wanted to get, and took selfies to send her way. At some point during this, however, was my highlight of the night. Dad had been showing off his hip flask prepped with his favourite whiskey. Now, I'm not a whiskey drinker. Rum is the superior spirit in my opinion. But the moment a new drink gets passed around, I get curious, and so I asked if I could try some. And when you drink from a hip flask, you can't half arse it. So I took a decent swig to get past the immediate burn in my mouth and catch the flavour behind it.

And Dana's dad laughed at me and said, "You really are your father's son, huh?"

My Progress
P-Shell

Our History In Colour

THE RAINBOW FLAG WAS created in 1978 in San Francisco by Gilbert Baker, an LGBT+ activist and vexillographer (flag maker). Made of eight coloured stripes, each colour denotes a specific meaning: pink for sex, red for life, and so on, with all eight colours symbolising a rainbow. In 1979, two of the colours, pink and turquoise, were dropped due to fabric availability, resulting in the six-colour flag we know and love today: red, orange, yellow, green, indigo, and violet.

In 2017, to recognise People of Colour, Philadelphia's Office of LGBT Affairs added the colours brown and black.

A year later, Daniel Quasar, a non-binary American artist, developed the Progress Flag. He added brown, black, white, pale pink, and pale blue to the original rainbow flag to visually embrace marginalised people of colour in the LGBT+ community, as well as the trans and non-binary community, and those living with HIV/AIDS. For Quasar, the arrow pointing to the right depicts forward movement, yet its position along the left edge highlights that progress is still needed.

My Life in Colour

Red. Without a doubt, my Nottingham Forest shirt. In its proudest splendour in Garibaldi red, with its iconic logo of a Sherwood Forest tree emerging from the wavy lines that depict the River Trent emblazoned across the left breast. It symbolises a pride in the city, my pride. The city in which I reside, the first place I felt able to call home and to be myself, to be accepted for who I am and not who I was or who I may become. The city where I met the love of my life, who is also a fan of the beautiful game as it happens, although we're sofa warriors as opposed to stadium troopers now. Regardless, watching them return to the Premiership this year was a moment of pure joy. The bliss came later!

Orange. My first encounter of the beautiful and elegant bird of paradise was in Los Angeles as we waited in line to enter Universal Studios. An appreciator of the beauty of flowers but not a lover, I was astounded by the sheer assault on my senses of this plant. Standing over four feet tall, these lush paddle-shaped leaves reminiscent of the banana plant were topped with the most astounding orange and blue petals, like the plumage of an exotic bird from halcyon days. Nothing as pure and as beautiful could exist in modern society. The fee to Universal was worth it just for that, which I have no doubt would baffle many a reader, but it was just so perfect, and it became our flower. Of course, the magic didn't end there. I got to kiss Shrek at Universal, even though I had my own princess by my side. She didn't mind. She got to kiss Donkey!

Yellow: Waking up at four in the morning to trudge the few hundred yards from our hotel in South Beach Miami to sit on the golden sands, awaiting the first glimpse of sunrise over the Atlantic Ocean, is my yellow. Such a mesmerising, buttery glow as it peeked above the horizon before showing its golden splendour and bathing us in its warmth. Following a rich and colourful breakfast of pancakes, eggs, berries, and melon, we set out on a leisurely 159-mile drive down the Florida Keys to our hotel in Key West. A long, stunning drive across island after island, crystal blue water on both sides, just beyond the lush green vegetation. Once there, we joined in the sunset celebrations, with vibrant music, captivating performers and colourful personage, and danced to a Latin beat. It seemed that everyone's heart was throbbing to the same rhythm. There was a collective silence as we all turned to the shore to watch the sun set slowly and languidly into the Gulf of Mexico. At that point, it was as if there were only two of us in the whole world, a shared moment which, although felt by hundreds of others, was unique to us.

Green: The land where it's always green, unless it's white: Scotland. Every day seems to have the potential for rain, and so the grass, the leaves, and the trees all rise to greet the pure, untainted moisture that is promised, the one that gives everything it touches its iridescent glow. Out in the middle of nowhere, a haven from any light pollution, we seek the hypnotic powers of the northern lights. The sun sets quickly over the horizon, and the greens of the day fade to the browns and greys of the evening before being swallowed completely by the darkness. We have a long wait until the temperature drops for optimum visibility, but we sit patiently, gazing in anticipation and hugging closely, wrapped in a blanket awaiting the unearthly spectacle. We didn't see it this time, but the journey wasn't wasted. We were together, it was our space, and no one else mattered. And as the clouds broke free in the sky, dozens of shooting stars streamed across the black canvas of the midnight sky. We both made a wish that we would be together forever or, at least as long as there are stars in the sky.

Indigo: Waves lapped at the side of the boat, Kitty Kat, as we bobbed in the Gulf of the Farallones, thirty miles east of the San Francisco coast. In search of blue whales, humpback whales, and orcas, we drifted aimlessly in the vibrant indigo waters set against the tableaux of the Farallon Islands. The islands, sometimes referred to by mariners as the Devil's Teeth Islands due to the many treacherous underwater landforms beneath the waves, glistened in the sun, emitting a purity only this watery wilderness could conjure up, one free from human violation. We weren't to be graced by the huge creatures, but we had the opportunity to see seals, sea lions, dolphins, puffins, cormorants, oystercatchers, and rock pigeons, including what appeared to be a distant relative of Roger, a frequent visitor to our Nottingham garden. It was a true assault of our senses: the vibrant indigo blue waters and white wave spume, which washed excitedly over our sun-kissed skin; the movement of the boat, jostling us from side to side, making us wish we hadn't eaten that day. The air itself was full and raw with the sounds of nature, the waves crashing, the seals barking and roaring, fortunately not culled by the silent approach of the great white shark that frequents these waters. And then, to be welcomed under the Golden Gate Bridge on our return to shore by the local ambassador, a sea lion named Bob, eagerly awaiting his daily fish treat courtesy of our guide and naturalist, Captain Tom.

Violet: We'd been to California and Florida and felt a sense of comfort and pride in who we are and the fact that we, two females, were still madly and truly in love with each other after over ten years together. Those far-off places were where we'd been accepted, but what about back home? It was time to get our dungarees on and visit the UK centre of Gaydom that is Brighton. Finding that we were the only curvy couple in a gay-run hotel amongst a sea of straights was quite disarming, but we soon became the novelty in this tourist tour of couples seeking the company of some of the exquisite creatures characteristic of the LGBT+ community. We kept it to friendly chats over breakfast, of course. Shopping in The Lanes, we sought out different and unique jewellery, something that captured our inner spirit. My wife gravitated to an aquamarine ring in a square titanium setting, which appeared to float in space. I homed in on the biggest, brightest amethyst, a cabochon-cut monstrosity embedded in a Celtic silver mount. It was so perfect and so me–I'm an extrovert, but this was bolder and brighter than would normally grace my digits. A stone once celebrated in myth and legend, its iridescence sparkled on my eternity finger in the light. We were happy with our treasures, just disappointed that our gayness wasn't as affirming as it had felt in San Francisco. But perhaps by then, we had moved on as a couple and had a contentedness and strength of being more than the sum of our parts.

Brown: Without a doubt, the colour that I see as I gaze into the chocolate velvety depths of my brown-eyed girl, my soulmate. The one who taught me to love but perhaps more importantly, how to be loved. From the very first moment we met, there were never any awkward silences, arguments, or regrets. We were safe in the knowledge that we had finally met the one we wished to share our lives with, fully and wholeheartedly. All the words, emotions, and feelings were clearly illustrated in our self-penned wedding vows: "This ring of gold is what we hold so dearly in our hearts. It speaks of truth, undying love, and how we'll never part. It has no end and no beginning; it's solid to the core. To be with you for all my life, I could wish for nothing more."

Black: The raven locks of my mother in her twenties and thirties will always be my vision of true black. Her hair tied up in a beehive, all silky and shiny, with a Mallen streak high above her left eye. A formidable character, full of love and pride for her only child but not quite able to fathom or accept the concept of same-sex relationships, or that women can love and marry women. An intense shame borne out of the thought of what others might think if they learned about her cherub. The years have moved on and tensions have eased, almost to an acceptance, but one wonders if this is the result of having less energy to endure, a recognition that times have changed, or a failing memory where what others think is no longer as important as it once so strongly was. Black still symbolises a loss that lingers. To have had the opportunity to share the joy and happiness of finding my soulmate with my mum would have meant the world to me.

White: White is the colour of my skin, at least in census terms. I think of myself more as a warm beige. I carry this colour of privilege with me wherever I go. It doesn't necessarily mean that I'm privileged in economic or financial terms, or that I'm not susceptible to the barriers imposed by society or the establishment. It simply means that by virtue of my skin colour, I'm not questioned for being me. I'm not racially profiled because of the paucity of melanin in my skin cells. I'm not judged and discriminated against for possessing a biological trait that was intended to protect us humans from the sun. Belonging to the LGBT+ family has had its ups and downs for me, some joyous, others heart-breaking, but how must it be for my siblings of colour? For disabled, gay women of colour? For those who are still close to their god but ostracised from their religion and/or their community? I am blessed by my white privilege but not complacent about my role in eradicating it.

Pale Pink: The colour associated with my birth, but one that I never completely aligned with. Proud, content, and comfortable to be a female throughout my years, yet still struggling with the concept that gender has to be fixed or the ideology that there are boys' jobs and girls' jobs, masculine things to do and feminine ways of being. I guess I rebelled against the status quo from a very early age, the frilly dresses, the curls in my hair, the bonnets, and furry hats. Like the time when I was about four years old, all dressed up and ready to go out to an event with my parents, hair curled in ringlets, beautiful pale lemon summer cotton dress, and shiny black patent leather shoes. But little P-Shell didn't want to go, so she climbed the stairs as fast as her little legs would carry her, went to the bathroom, and stuck her head under the tap. Clothing absolutely drenched, soaking wet hair, not a curl in sight. Alas, the shoes were fine and matched perfectly with my pale blue denim dungarees. Oh, how I giggled all night...to myself, of course. I was adorable regardless, and soon my folly was forgotten. Until I reached adulthood, when it became an amusing tale to tell. So, do I like pink now, you may ask? Only when it's champagne, darling.

Pale Blue: A recognition that I possess traits considered by some to be masculine. For example, I love cars, and I mean nice cars: fast, powerful, and expensive ones—none of your poser nonsense though. I can even tell you the difference between a V6 and a V8 engine in more detail than your average male and have never been fooled when sent for a left-hand screwdriver or a triple lay overhead manifold sprocket.

Remember the Drifter chocolate adverts from the early nineties? If you've never seen one, try Google. I, like some men, enjoy formidable tools such as hammer drills, angle grinders, and power saws, but only when I can be a*sed to do so. And washing the car? Well, with two women in the house, someone has to draw the short straw and fortunately, that's not me! After all, I do have to share the glamour of some duties society says belong to men.

My True Colours

So this is my progress, my journey laid out before you in glorious technicolour, as illustrated through the colours of the Quasar Flag.

Throughout my journey, I've celebrated the good and survived the bad, and I wear the scars that I've accumulated along the way as badges of honour. Fighting for freedom, which the rainbow flag is all about, is a battle, a battle I unashamedly commit to in collaboration with the community that embraced me as one of their own. It's true that, with time, things can and often do change, and the progress made within society over the last twenty years is reflected in my journey. But I'm increasingly mindful that there's so much more we need to do collectively in the struggle for true equality.

Each colour of our flag signifies a unique and vital part of what has shaped me into the proud gay woman I am today. The vivid colours and what they signify will never change for me, as they're imprinted on my being, yet their hue grows stronger and deeper with time.

What's Your Story?

Global Wordsmiths, CIC, provides an all-encompassing service for all writers, ranging from basic proofreading and cover design to development editing, typesetting, and eBook services. A major part of our work is charity and community focused, delivering writing projects to under-served and under-represented groups across Nottinghamshire, giving voice to the voiceless and visibility to the unseen.

To learn more about what we offer, visit: www.globalwords.co.uk

A selection of anthologies by Global Words Press:
Desire, Love, Identity: with the National Justice Museum
Times Past: with The Workhouse, National Trust
World At War: Farmilo Primary School
Times Past: Young at Heart with AGE UK
In Different Shoes: Stories of Trans Lives

Self-published authors working with Global Wordsmiths:
E.V. Bancroft
Valden Bush
Addison M Conley
Helena Harte
Lee Haven
Iona Kane
Karen Klyne
AJ Mason
James Merrick
Emma Nichols
Robyn Nyx
Simon Smalley
Brey Willows

Butterworth Books

Let Love Be Enough by Robyn Nyx
When a killer sets her sights on her target, is there any stopping her?
Available on Amazon (ASIN B09YMMZ8XC)

Lyrics of Life by Brey Willows
Sometimes the only way to heal someone's heart is a song from you own.
Coming June 2023 (ISBN 9781915009265)

An Art to Love by Helena Harte
Second chances are an art form.
Available from Amazon (ASIN B0B1CD8Y42)

Caribbean Dreams by Karen Klyne
When love sails into your life, do you climb aboard?
Available from Amazon (ASIN B09M41PYM9)

Nero by Valden Bush
Will her destiny reunite her with the love of her life?
Available from Amazon (B09BXN8VTZ)

Of Light and Love by E.V. Bancroft
The deepest shadows paint the brightest love.
Available from Amazon (B0B64KJ3NP)

The Helion Band *by AJ Mason*
Rose's only crime was to show kindness to her royal mistress...
Available from Amazon (ASIN B09YM6TYFQ)

That Boy of Yours Wants Looking At by Simon Smalley
A gloriously colourful and heart-rending memoir.
Available from Amazon (ASIN B09HSN9NM8)

Judge Me, Judge Me Not by James Merrick
A memoir of one gay man's battle against the world and himself.
Available from Amazon (ASIN B09CLK91N5)

LesFic Eclectic Volume Three edited by Robyn Nyx
Special edition raising funds for the DEC Ukrainian appeal: available from Amazon (ASIN B09V39LW2W)

Printed in Great Britain
by Amazon

86893910R00109